Fine Arts, Music and Literature

Measuring the Arts

Research Agendas and a System Map of How Art Works

FINE ARTS, MUSIC AND LITERATURE

Additional books in this series can be found on Nova's website
under the Series tab.

Additional e-books in this series can be found on Nova's website
under the e-book tab.

FINE ARTS, MUSIC AND LITERATURE

MEASURING THE ARTS

RESEARCH AGENDAS AND A SYSTEM MAP OF HOW ART WORKS

KATIE C. O'CONNELL
AND
DAVID E. MYRICK
EDITORS

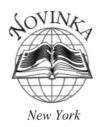

New York

Copyright © 2013 by Nova Science Publishers, Inc.

All rights reserved. No part of this book may be reproduced, stored in a retrieval system or transmitted in any form or by any means: electronic, electrostatic, magnetic, tape, mechanical photocopying, recording or otherwise without the written permission of the Publisher.

For permission to use material from this book please contact us:
Telephone 631-231-7269; Fax 631-231-8175
Web Site: http://www.novapublishers.com

NOTICE TO THE READER

The Publisher has taken reasonable care in the preparation of this book, but makes no expressed or implied warranty of any kind and assumes no responsibility for any errors or omissions. No liability is assumed for incidental or consequential damages in connection with or arising out of information contained in this book. The Publisher shall not be liable for any special, consequential, or exemplary damages resulting, in whole or in part, from the readers' use of, or reliance upon, this material. Any parts of this book based on government reports are so indicated and copyright is claimed for those parts to the extent applicable to compilations of such works.

Independent verification should be sought for any data, advice or recommendations contained in this book. In addition, no responsibility is assumed by the publisher for any injury and/or damage to persons or property arising from any methods, products, instructions, ideas or otherwise contained in this publication.

This publication is designed to provide accurate and authoritative information with regard to the subject matter covered herein. It is sold with the clear understanding that the Publisher is not engaged in rendering legal or any other professional services. If legal or any other expert assistance is required, the services of a competent person should be sought. FROM A DECLARATION OF PARTICIPANTS JOINTLY ADOPTED BY A COMMITTEE OF THE AMERICAN BAR ASSOCIATION AND A COMMITTEE OF PUBLISHERS.

Additional color graphics may be available in the e-book version of this book.

Library of Congress Cataloging-in-Publication Data

ISBN: 978-1-62618-269-1

Published by Nova Science Publishers, Inc. † *New York*

CONTENTS

Preface   **vii**

Chapter 1   How Art Works: The National Endowment
for the Arts' Five-Year Research Agenda,
with a System Map and Measurement Model   **1**
National Endowment for the Arts

Chapter 2   How Art Works: The National Endowment
for the Arts' Five-Year Research Agenda,
with a System Map and Measurement Model,
Appendix A and Appendix B   **59**
National Endowment for the Arts

Chapter 3   The Arts and Human Development: Framing
a National Research Agenda for the Arts, Lifelong
Learning and Individual Well-Being   **81**
*Gay Hanna, Michael Patterson, Judy Rollins
and Andrea Sherman*

Index   **121**

PREFACE

This book examines the National Endowment for the Arts'(NEA) five-year agenda for research and provides a conceptual frame for planning and assessing research priorities so that the NEA can improve its ability to meet a core goal: to promote knowledge and understanding about the contributions of the arts. Concurrent with that process, the agency embarked on a series of in-depth dialogues, through interviews, webinars, and workshops, with leading thinkers in a variety of fields and sectors not exclusive to the arts. The goal of those consultations was to establish a feasible, testable, hypothesis for understanding how art works in American life. The result of the NEA's deliberations and expert consultations was a system map and measurement model that can guide the NEA's annual milestone development process as part of its five-year research agenda.

Chapter 1 – This document sets forth the National Endowment for the Arts' five-year agenda for research, but it does more than that. It provides a conceptual frame for planning and assessing research priorities so that the NEA can improve its ability to meet a core goal: *To Promote Knowledge and Understanding about the Contributions of the Arts.*

This goal appears in the NEA's Strategic Plan for FY 2012–2016. The plan charges the Arts Endowment's Office of Research and Analysis (ORA) with drafting a five-year research agenda with annual milestones for reporting to the White House Office of Management and Budget, Congress, and the American public. Thus, in 2011 ORA developed operating principles for the research agenda and presented them for feedback from a variety of stakeholders. (To view the presentation, visit arts.gov/research/Service-orgs-meeting.html.)

Concurrent with that process, the agency embarked on a series of in-depth dialogues —through interviews, webinars, and workshops—with leading thinkers in a variety of fields and sectors not exclusive to the arts. The goal of those consultations was to establish a feasible, testable hypothesis for understanding how art works in American life.

The rationale for this approach was two-fold. First, much of the NEA's past research on arts and culture has responded directly to the availability of specific datasets; to that extent, such research has been largely descriptive and reactive, rather than theory-driven and pro-active. The second reason for attempting to outline "how art works" is that a theory of change would enable us better to study the arts as a complete system, and thus allow us more clearly to define the arts' "value" and "impact." Understanding those terms is crucial if the NEA is to track progress on achieving its strategic outcome for all research activity: *Evidence of the Value and Impact of the Arts is Expanded and Promoted.*

The result of the NEA's deliberations and expert consultations was a system map and measurement model (shown in Sections Two and Three of this chapter) that can guide ORA's annual milestone development process as part of its five-year research agenda. This chapter (in Section Four) lists priority

research projects that have emerged from ORA's own operating principles, but it also aligns those projects with key variables identified by the system map. The map organizes the research in a way that permits greater exploration of gaps and opportunities.

The NEA's Office of Research and Analysis is indebted to a long list of bibliographical resources, interview subjects, and workshop and webinar participants for assisting its pursuit of a theory-driven map and measurement model to guide future work. In particular, ORA relied on the expertise of Tony Siesfeld, Andrew Blau, Lance Potter, Don Derosby, Jessica Gheiler, and the Monitor Group. We now welcome broader public engagement with scholars, arts practitioners, and policy-makers so that the chapter can provoke fresh research and insights about the value and impact of the arts in America.

Chapter 2 – Appendix A and Appendix B for chapter 1 - How Art Works: The National Endowment for the Arts' Five-Year Research Agenda, with a System Map and Measurement Model,

Chapter 3 – Human development describes a complex web of factors affecting the health and well-being of individuals across the lifespan. Together, these factors yield cognitive and behavioral outcomes that can shape the social and economic circumstances of individuals, their levels of creativity and productivity, and overall quality of life.

Increasingly in the 21st century, U.S. policy leaders in health and education have recognized a need for strategies and interventions to address "the whole person." They have urged a more integrated approach to policy development—one that can reach Americans at various stages of their lives, across generations, and in multiple learning contexts.

The arts are ideally suited to promote this integrated approach. In study after study, arts participation and arts education have been associated with improved cognitive, social, and behavioral outcomes in individuals *across the lifespan*: in early childhood, in adolescence and young adulthood, and in later years. The studies include:

- Neuroscience research showing strong connections between arts learning and improved cognitive development;
- Small comparison group studies revealing the arts' contributions to school-readiness in early childhood;
- Longitudinal data analyses demonstrating positive academic and social outcomes for at-risk teenagers who receive arts education; and
- Several studies reporting improvements in cognitive function and self-reported quality of life for older adults who engage in the arts and creative activities, compared to those who do not.

This emerging body of evidence appears to support a need for greater integration of arts activities into health and educational programs for children, youth, and older adults. Yet further research is necessary so that policy-makers and practitioners can understand the pathways and processes by which the arts affect human development, thereby enhancing the efficacy of arts-based practices in optimizing health and educational outcomes for Americans of all ages.

In: Measuring the Arts
Editors: K. O'Connell and D. Myrick

ISBN: 978-1-62618-269-1
© 2013 Nova Science Publishers, Inc.

Chapter 1

HOW ART WORKS: THE NATIONAL ENDOWMENT FOR THE ARTS' FIVE-YEAR RESEARCH AGENDA, WITH A SYSTEM MAP AND MEASUREMENT MODEL[*]

National Endowment for the Arts

PREFACE

This document sets forth the National Endowment for the Arts' five-year agenda for research, but it does more than that. It provides a conceptual frame for planning and assessing research priorities so that the NEA can improve its ability to meet a core goal: *To Promote Knowledge and Understanding about the Contributions of the Arts.*

This goal appears in the NEA's Strategic Plan for FY 2012–2016. The plan charges the Arts Endowment's Office of Research and Analysis (ORA) with drafting a five-year research agenda with annual milestones for reporting to the White House Office of Management and Budget, Congress, and the American public. Thus, in 2011 ORA developed operating principles for the research agenda and presented them for feedback from a variety of

---

[*] This is an edited, reformatted and augmented version of a National Endowment for the Arts Report, dated September 2012.

2   National Endowment for the Arts

stakeholders. (To view the presentation, visit arts.gov/research/Service-orgs-meeting.html.)

Concurrent with that process, the agency embarked on a series of in-depth dialogues —through interviews, webinars, and workshops—with leading thinkers in a variety of fields and sectors not exclusive to the arts. The goal of those consultations was to establish a feasible, testable hypothesis for understanding how art works in American life.

The rationale for this approach was two-fold. First, much of the NEA's past research on arts and culture has responded directly to the availability of specific datasets; to that extent, such research has been largely descriptive and reactive, rather than theory-driven and pro-active. The second reason for attempting to outline "how art works" is that a theory of change would enable us better to study the arts as a complete system, and thus allow us more clearly to define the arts' "value" and "impact." Understanding those terms is crucial if the NEA is to track progress on achieving its strategic outcome for all research activity: *Evidence of the Value and Impact of the Arts is Expanded and Promoted.*

The result of the NEA's deliberations and expert consultations was a system map and measurement model (shown in Sections Two and Three of this chapter) that can guide ORA's annual milestone development process as part of its five-year research agenda. This chapter (in Section Four) lists priority
research projects that have emerged from ORA's own operating principles, but it also aligns those projects with key variables identified by the system map. The map organizes the research in a way that permits greater exploration of gaps and opportunities.

The NEA's Office of Research and Analysis is indebted to a long list of bibliographical resources, interview subjects, and workshop and webinar participants for assisting its pursuit of a theory-driven map and measurement model to guide future work. In particular, ORA relied on the expertise of Tony Siesfeld, Andrew Blau, Lance Potter, Don Derosby, Jessica Gheiler, and the Monitor Group. We now welcome broader public engagement with scholars, arts practitioners, and policy-makers so that the chapter can provoke fresh research and insights about the value and impact of the arts in America.

Sunil Iyengar
Director, Research and Analysis
National Endowment for the Arts

BACKGROUND NOTE ON GOALS AND METHODS

Why a System Map?

This chapter stems from a collaborative research inquiry into the nature and consequences of art in American life. Although it culminates in a research agenda for the National Endowment for the Arts, the document also proposes a way for the nation's cultural researchers, arts practitioners, policy-makers, and the general public to view, analyze, and discuss the arts as a dynamic, complex system.

It is characteristic of complex systems that they afford many points of entry and many different vantages, according to the user. Such systems also have many moving parts, which often interact in mysterious ways. It is frequently the case that examining one or more of these parts in isolation will fail to reveal the cumulative effect of the system or its emergent properties.

A well-established technique for managing this complexity, for the purpose of analysis, is to create a system map. The tool has been used widely in commerce to understand markets, value chains, the birth of new sectors, and how information flows within the walls of a business. System maps have figured in a variety of fields and sectors, ranging from neuroscience and public health to the evolution of economies.

The arts *are* a dynamic, complex system. They have a rich intellectual history of arguments and counter-arguments. Thus, their inputs, core components, and impacts are ideally suited for system mapping.

A system map of "how art works" can provide an opportunity to organize recurring themes and concepts. At a time when robust data collection and reporting drives the ability of most U.S. sectors to define themselves and demonstrate their worth, such a map can be all the more valuable. It allows people from diverse backgrounds and viewpoints to arrive at a shared understanding of how the system works, what are its key elements and relationships, and which external factors can alter the system's efficacy. It provides a cartography of current research and exposes gaps in knowledge. Beyond these merits, a system map offers a blueprint for future measurement goals and strategies, suggesting which variables are critical to study for the purpose of communicating impact.

Researchers, policy-makers, and practitioners in the arts sector have had no shortage of ideas for articulating the arts' potential impacts on individuals and communities. Many of those concepts have flowed from original analyses of existing datasets, including studies conducted or commissioned by the

National Endowment for the Arts. Researchers from a host of disciplines have contributed to an extensive literature attempting to describe core components of the U.S. arts ecosystem, or to quantify the arts' impact from a variety of perspectives.

Some of the most compelling research has originated in non-arts specialties: cognitive neuroscience, for example, with its discoveries about the arts' role in shaping learning-related outcomes; labor economics, with its lessons about the arts' bearing on national and local productivity; urban planning fieldwork that seeks to understand the arts as a marker of community vitality; and psychological studies that posit the arts' relationship to health and well-being.

The present chapter begins with the assumption that despite such pioneering efforts, the NEA's Office of Research and Analysis would benefit from a visual interpretation of "how art works." The model should outline a rational, defensible theory of change, and it should carry direct implications for measurement.

Another assumption behind this chapter is that although many lenses have been applied to understand the arts as a discrete ecosystem, or to measure the various types of impact it produces along different dimensions, seldom has a unified theory been brought to investigate these questions.

Before embarking on a project of this formidable scope, it was necessary to start from a humbler place. The project involved literature reviews and consultations with a broad group of people highly accomplished in their fields, not all of which were arts-related. They came from the academic, government, not-for-profit, and commercial sectors, spanning a breadth of artistic, scientific, and media disciplines, and they participated in a string of interviews, workshops, webinars, and online exchanges. The process involved "rapid prototyping" to produce a map, variables, and definitions that formed the basis for those in the chapter. (Go here for a description of the consultation process, a list of participants, and a selective bibliography: arts.gov/research/How-Art-Works/ index.html.)

What this chapter does *not* do is attempt to resolve longstanding points of contention in the arts. Nor does the system map claim to be definitive. Rather, it articulates a theory for understanding how art works, offers an integrative and holistic map for organizing existing research, and illustrates what the National Endowment for the Arts is doing to clarify parts of the map so we might better comprehend the entire system and its implications for the quality of life for all Americans.

We have organized this chapter into four sections: an overview of our theory of "how art works" (Section One); a detailed description of the system map and its components (Section Two); a measurement model for the map, inclusive of component variables, definitional questions, and methodological challenges (Section Three); and the NEA's planned research projects over a five-year period (Section Four).

To a large extent, the *How Art Works* system map reflects the strengths, limitations, and potential of existing research on the arts. Alternatives to the map—or future iterations—may generate even better research questions and methodologies to explore the nature of art, its contributions to human and societal development, and its place in American life.

SECTION ONE: ESTABLISHING A THEORY OF HOW ART WORKS AS A SYSTEM

Historically, generations of artists, philosophers, critics, and social scientists have struggled to define the role and impacts of art in terms of public value. They have asked questions as fundamental as: What *is* art? What is the nature of an artistic experience? What factors and conditions contribute to that experience, and how do they manifest in individuals and societies? What benefits do the arts confer, how, and to whom, and how might those effects be better known?

Such questions propelled this project, which has generated a system map of art's impacts on quality of life, an analysis of the system's key variables and how they might be measured, and a conceptual basis for presenting and reviewing the NEA's five-year research agenda.

The project entailed a substantive literature review (more than 150 documents ranging from academic research studies to data sets) and a series of consultations with a broad spectrum of "experts." We use the term expansively: our experts came from the arts, from disciplines focused on the well-being of communities and individuals (e.g., demographers, psychologists, politicians and policy experts, economists, and industry executives), and from adjacent disciplines that endeavor to map and understand other complex, dynamic systems (e.g., weather, public health, Type II diabetes, and the theory of system dynamics). We sought informed judgment from various perspectives as we laid out key issues and then worked together to map a system of the arts and their impacts.

After 11 months and a series of collaborative working sessions, we produced a map that attempts to synthesize main elements of the system and their relationships to each other.[1] Our underlying hypothesis is that engagement in art contributes to quality of life. Quality of life contributes to society's capacity to invent, create, and express itself. This capacity contributes back to art, both directly and indirectly. When the system works, arts engagement expands and deepens, quality of life is enhanced, and the creative capacity of a society increases.

At the individual level, a person who engages in art— who creates, witnesses, is made angry by, or is enraptured by art—has the possibility of being changed. These changes are not certain, and most often are subtle. Over many instances of engagement, with different art or with the same art many times (or both), there is a good chance that a person's viewpoint and capacity for encountering other experiences will change. Over many people, over time, such changes can be profound. They can manifest as differences in people's cognitive, social, and emotional development. Engagement in art can expand the perspectives a person can take, deepen one's appreciation of things new and familiar, facilitate or enhance a feeling of spirituality, and lead to a sense of connection that was not originally present.

Within a community—a collection of people bound by some common element, be it geography, history, an area of interest, or some other shared characteristic—engaging in art can foster a sense of identity and belonging. It can promote and signal cultural vitality and communal values such as a tolerance of diversity and an openness to questions.[2]These communal values are ties that bind. At their best, such ties contribute to unity, identity, a sense of solidarity, higher levels of civic engagement, and ultimately the expectation of the right to culture. But these ties also can be exclusive, serving to reinforce a "right" and a "wrong" way of participating in a group.

Somewhat different from this community benefit are the economic benefits of art, both direct and indirect. This variable has been much investigated lately, with some studies purporting that geographically bound communities where artists have settled tend to produce higher real estate values, more tourism, and the growth of entertainment industries. In other words, arts engagement produces local economic activity.

Most directly, both the artist and the buyer gain through the exchange. The artist—and gallery or theater or other venue, if one is involved—earns income, and the patron gets artwork or an arts experience that both pleases and enriches. And, in the case of a tangible piece of art, the work may be sold and bought in the future. There are also indirect economic benefits.

Maybe through local policy and support, through the availability of inexpensive space that can be used as an artist's studio, or through the appeal of sharing a community of kindred souls, artists concentrate in a given area. Arts patrons frequenting the area may spur local revenue growth through food and drink purchases, hotel stays, and tourism spending. Not all artists benefit, and some may be forced to move on for less expensive space or some other reason, but the long term effect is that the neighborhood is now economically better off.

These benefits "talk to each other." They feed each other. A more vibrant community is one in which businesses are likely to want to operate. An active business life will enhance the community, and attract more people.

We hypothesize that these individual and community benefits of art represent its primary and most measurable contributions. When people engage in art, they themselves may change and "grow," they and their communities can become more vital, and the economic benefits to artists and the overall market can increase and accrue. Art contributes to and enriches the overall quality of life.

Much more indirectly, a healthy and robust engagement in the arts can raise the aptitude of a society for invention, creativity, and expression. Although the aptitude itself may be difficult to witness directly, it can be seen in the creation of new forms and outlets for expression. A contemporary example of this phenomenon is the combination of digital video, easy to-use editing software, and the Internet, all of which gave rise to YouTube, Myspace, and other places where a wide range of people are able to post their own creative expressions. A more fundamental instance of the capacity of our society to innovate and to express ideas is in the exercise of freedom of speech.

Our societal capacity to innovate and to express ideas can lead to support for arts infrastructure (e.g., government funding, or grants or other support from foundations, businesses, and individuals). It can result also in stronger commitments to formal and informal instruction in both the creation and appreciation of art. Arts infrastructure provides the financial support, materials, and human resources necessary for arts participation and arts creation, while education and training provide important knowledge and skills.

Beyond training and opportunity, something in human nature—an impulse to create and to express— fuels the artist, the creation of art, and ongoing arts engagement. Engagement in art contributes to an enhanced quality of life. As quality of life improves, more arts engagement occurs, strengthening a society's capacity to express ideas and to create. As this societal capacity increases, even greater levels of arts engagement can result directly and indirectly. Thus, when the system works, it builds itself and leads to healthier, more productive outcomes.

As a simplification of the real world, the system described here is inherently imperfect. The system sits in a wider system that influences individuals, communities, our economy and our very society. But in the system here described, art is central, though its impacts may be subtle.

In dialogue with experts from various backgrounds, we found that we could articulate a map of this complex, dynamic system linking arts participation, quality of life, and broad capabilities in our society. Our map depicts a Theory of Change for art—providing insight into how, why, and when arts engagement enhances the lives of individuals and communities.

The map reflects several key assumptions that arose from this collaborative research project. For example:

- Arts engagement—creating art or otherwise experiencing it—is at the heart of how art works. Art matters. It is an essential contributing factor to health, happiness, and prosperity.
- The raw fuel needed to keep the system going is the human impulse to create and express.
- Benefits can accrue separately to individuals and communities, and these benefits are not all equally distributed. Nor are they always reliably present.
- Arts engagement makes important contributions to the broad capacity of our society to invent and express itself.

The system map helps put long-standing controversies and disputes into a context that allows multiple perspectives to exist. It provides what Keats called "negative capability"—the ability to imagine the system without having to resolve apparently contradictory aspects. For instance, in the current map:

- Art can be an artifact, an action, or an ongoing process. It can be restricted to "high art" or expanded to "popular art." It can refer to one or more art forms. Nevertheless, how one sets the boundaries and limits to these concepts will determine which impacts can be evaluated. In this system, moreover, art does have to be a human endeavor, the invention and expression of a person.
- There are a multitude of individual-level and community-level outcomes associated with arts engagement. None is privileged (in the

sense that one is more important or more valuable than others), not all need be present in every circumstance, and the outcomes may register subjectively or objectively. Our system anticipates many subtle influences of arts engagement, over time and differentially over people.

- Art contributes to the greater quality of life of individuals and communities. Our single biggest measurement challenge will be to identify quality-of-life outcomes that can be attributed exclusively to arts engagement.

The system map provides an integrative and holistic model for organizing research to measure the arts' impacts. In Section Four of this chapter, we locate the NEA's planned and ongoing projects on the map. This exercise reveals potential areas that might be underrepresented in the agency's current research portfolio. In the same way, the nation's larger body of research on art's impacts can be organized by the system map, showing where distinct areas of research can be brought together for new insight.

This map is a beginning, not the end. It should provoke conversation, debate, and research. The results of these exchanges will help deepen and enrich the map, making it a better and more faithful representation of the complex, dynamic system of art's impacts.

As it currently stands, the map can be used to "explain" how art works as a system, and to provide a basis for planning future research.

SECTION TWO: MAPPING THE SYSTEM OF HOW ART WORKS

Overview

To tell the story of *How Art Works,* the NEA's Office of Research and Analysis and the strategy consulting firm Monitor Institute engaged citizens representing a wide range of shaping experiences and perspectives— including artists and non-artists, academics, policy-makers, and business people—to develop a common view of the relationship between art and individual and community outcomes. This series of exchanges produced a system map of art and its impacts (see Illustration 1).

What is this map? It is an abstract representation of the interplay among:

- Arts participation, inclusive of arts creation;
- The artist, the artwork, and audience;
- How arts participation influences the lives of individuals and their communities; and
- How individuals and their communities influence artists and their work.

The system map we created is a community effort, reflecting a series of discussions, literature searches, and interviews. (Go here for a description of the consultation process, a list of participants, and a selective bibliography: arts.gov/research/How-Art-Works/ index.html.)

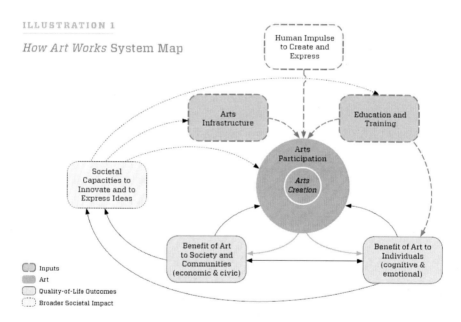

ILLUSTRATION 1

How Art Works System Map

The map is both very simple and extremely complicated. At its simplest, it says that with motivation and opportunity, a person (the artist) conceives of and expresses an idea. This idea, when it reaches another person, has an impact. This impact may be seen within the individual who engaged with the artwork, within the community, and/or in an economic exchange. This impact flows to the greater society, influencing its creative capacity, as well as its means and ability for expression. The impact also flows back to the artist, directly in some instances (e.g., the artist sells a work of art) and indirectly through education, infrastructure, and society's general embrace of creativity and freedom of expression.

Dig a layer deeper into the map and it reveals more complexity. For instance, the question of who has the "right" to call a work a piece of art—the artist, the audience, or an informed third party—does not need an answer in the system map. All these perspectives are possible but no one perspective is privileged. Choosing one perspective influences which effects are observed, and at what level of magnitude. Likewise, the distinction between high and low art need not be made, as both are accommodated in this map. But changing the "breadth" of the definition of art will change the number of people engaged, and therefore how many people can be affected and how large (relative to the total population) the impacts are. Whether or not our definition includes publishing, radio, and/or movies, for example, strongly influences how many people engage with art—and, in particular, how much direct economic benefit accrues from art.

One risk of system mapping is the tendency to try to accommodate everything within the map. To limit this risk in the context of *How Art Works,* we have assumed that a work of art is **an act of creative expression done within the confines of a set of known or emerging practices and precedence that is intended to communicate richly to others** (e.g., a symphony performance, a teenager's final art project, and a grandmother's crochet practice). As we are interested specifically in the impact of art on individuals and communities, in our definition we stipulate that at least one person other than the artist is required to engage with the work.

In addition to depicting the story of *How Art Works,* the map implies a number of things about measuring art's impact. We will turn to those implications presently. First, let's tour the map.

The *How Art Works* system consists of four parts: inputs; art itself; quality-of-life outcomes (first-order outcomes); and broader societal impacts (second-order outcomes). Primary inputs are factors and forces providing foundational structure to artists and arts participation. Art comes in the form of both artifacts and experiences. Quality-of-life outcomes are primary and more immediate effects of art and arts participation. Broader societal impacts result from quality-of life outcomes.

System Components

Human Impulse to Create and Express
This is the primary motive that powers the system: the basic drive for virtually all humans across all time to express themselves at some point, to make a creative mark.

How Art Works takes *Human Impulse to Create and Express* as the animating force behind arts participation (which can be to create something, to express something, or to receive or interact with the creative expression of another), and all of its social consequences; accordingly, it is a constant in the system, and a fundamentally different type of input from *Arts Infrastructure* and *Education and Training.* This impulse is a necessary but insufficient condition for arts engagement. Arts engagement requires opportunity. Much of the context for this opportunity is provided by the inputs below.

Inputs
System inputs enable a context for arts creation and arts participation. In this system, there are two broad inputs:

- *Arts Infrastructure* refers to the institutions, places, spaces, and formal and informal social support systems that facilitate the creation and consumption of art.
- *Education and Training* refers to the standards, best practices, knowledge models, and skills that inform artistic expression on the one hand, and consumption of art on the other. *Education and Training* spans the spectrum of formal and informal instruction, from YouTube and street jam sessions, to K-12 and adult arts education, to apprenticeships and conservatory training.

Combined, *Human Impulse to Create and Express, Arts Infrastructure,* and *Education and Training* lend the context and motivation on which artistic endeavors, audience experiences, and any resulting benefits are built.

Art
Art, especially arts engagement, sits at the heart of the system. To understand it as intended here, we need to acknowledge that Art includes artistic acts (arts creation) and the consumption of those outputs (arts participation). Regarded this way—and in the context of the map—Art is both noun and verb; it is the thing and the act of producing and experiencing it.

- The act of producing, interpreting, curating, and otherwise experiencing art is *Arts Participation.*
- In the system map, we call out *Arts Creation* as one essential aspect of *Arts Participation.* The agent of *Arts Creation* is the artist, broadly and inclusively defined as a person who expresses herself or himself within the confines of a set of known or emerging practices and precedence, with the intention of communicating richly to others. Art, in this system, is created by someone with intention.

Quality-of-Life Outcomes (First-Order Outcomes)

Quality-of-life outcomes are community and individual benefits derived from interacting with the arts. These benefits can have a positive or negative value in the context of the system map (i.e., you can have "more" or "less" economic, social and community, or individual benefits). And because of demographic heterogeneity across the United States, it is possible for more benefits to accrue to one individual, group, institution, or community than to others. We have grouped quality-of-life outcomes into two broad categories.

- The first is the *Benefit of Art to Individuals,* which refers to the cognitive, emotional, behavioral, and physiological effects that arts participation can produce in individuals, including transformations in thinking, social skills, and character development over time.[3]
- The second is *Benefit of Art to Society and Communities.* This outcome refers to:
  - The role that art plays as an agent of cultural vitality, a contributor to sense of place and sense of belonging, a vehicle for transfer of values and ideals, and a promoter of political dialogue.[4]
  - The role it plays as a source of economic benefit. This is both the direct income derived from the arts (e.g., the price paid for an arts experience or artifact of the commercial arts) and the indirect financial returns of the arts (e.g., increases in the value of real estate, or benefits to the hospitality industry).[5]

Discussions of the value of art invariably seek to highlight a portion of one of these factors, often at the exclusion of other parts. Our research in developing an integrated system suggests that the civic and economic components of art's benefit to communities and the emotional and cognitive components of art's benefit to individuals are best acknowledged at all points

14   National Endowment for the Arts

in time and that the particular value of one type of benefit over the other can be understood only in unique circumstances. Recent arts policy and case-making for the arts has overemphasized the critical value of art's direct and indirect economic impacts on society. Although those analyses and resulting numbers certainly matter and are attractive because of their concrete nature, our research suggests that the other individual and community values of art—if they were more directly quantifiable—in all likelihood far outweigh the measurable financial values of the arts.

Broader Societal Impacts (Second-Order Outcomes)

To complete the systems perspective of how art works, we need to take into consideration a final category of variables we label here as broader societal impact. The overall impact is *Societal Capacities to Innovate and to Express Ideas.* But a more detailed system map (see Illustration 3 in Section Three of this chapter) reveals two attendant types of outcomes. One is *New Forms of Self-Expression,* which reflects new ideas and new idioms, and the other is *Outlets for Creative Expression,* which reflects how technological changes are altering the sources and reach of creative expression. These variables are downstream from our core quality-of-life indicators; yet they are essential to understanding how the arts can shape broader life experiences of Americans.

- *Societal Capacities to Innovate and to Express Ideas* refers to the ability of community members to "develop, design, or create new applications, ideas, relationships, systems, or products"—individually and collectively.[6]
- *New Forms of Self-Expression* (see Illustration 3, Section Three) refers to the emerging methods, techniques, and materials we have for conveying emotional states and ideas, from new art modalities to data visualization.
- *Outlets for Creative Expression* (see Illustration 3, Section Three) refers to the platforms that support these new forms of expression, such as YouTube, Myspace and Facebook. New outlets and forms of expression not only become new media in which artists can express themselves—they also enable more individuals to become artists, forcing us to alter the ways we think about art forms and fields.

Our capacity to innovate and to express ideas, and its links to forms and outlets for expression, also point up a core liberty within our society: freedom of expression. This freedom requires certain individual- and community-level attitudes that are facilitated by the arts: for example, the courage to express oneself and a tolerance of new ideas and vehicles for creative expression. The system map implies a link between arts participation and our ability, opportunity, and likelihood to express ourselves freely.

The benefits of these broader societal impacts spill over to creative problem-solving as it applies to a whole range of other endeavors, from the sciences to design and mass media. Regarded this way, the broader societal impacts of the arts are both greater in scope and more difficult to track directly back to the arts as classically defined. As we will highlight below, these impacts interact with "system multipliers," influencing society well beyond arts participation.

By explicitly acknowledging the impacts of *Societal Capacities to Innovate and to Express Ideas, New Forms of Self-Expression,* and *Outlets for Creative Expression* as part of an expanded system map, we establish critical ties between the arts and the pollination that takes place between the arts and the highly innovative (and often commercial) spaces that have birthed phenomena as disparate as self-publishing through blogging, socially networked arts funding engines (e.g., Kickstarter), media arts-initiated social or political activism, and open-source software platforms.

Broader societal impacts in the system also provide essential links back to *Arts Infrastructure, Education and Training,* and *Arts Participation.* They complete feedback loops that we know exist in the real world; core inputs feed artistic production, artistic production feeds quality of life, quality of life enables the *Societal Capacities to Innovate and to Express Ideas,* and this creative capacity reinforces basic inputs.

System Multipliers

Multipliers are factors and forces that broadly influence particular states of the arts system at points in time, and may act through many system variables, even simultaneously. To understand the state of the system at any point in time, we need to take stock of how the multipliers are affecting it. By isolating these five essential multipliers, we are able to characterize changes to the system as time passes. We propose five primary multipliers: Markets and Subsidies; Politics; Technology; Demographics and Cultural Traditions; and Space and Time (see Illustration 2).

1. Markets and Subsidies: Refers to the supply-and-demand factors outside the system, including policy mechanisms that direct money and resources to different parts of the arts universe at different points in time.

2. Politics: Refers to the public dialogue and legislative practices that help set the rules of the game through which arts are acknowledged, rewarded, and occasionally vilified.

3. Technology: Refers to human-made devices with the capability to magnify impact, collapse distance, and distort time. These devices sometimes affect the arts by making new forms and outlets for expression possible, e.g., digital media and basic tech tools supporting new crafts, or by transforming existing expressions into new modalities that can be broadly distributed and consumed at will.

4. Demographics and Cultural Traditions: Refers to the size and composition of human populations over time. This multiplier captures the critical influence of emigration and immigration, the bulging population of cities, and the simultaneous shrinking population in the countryside. It captures complexities associated with the resulting cultural mash-ups and cross-pollination of artistic forms, and group-based preferences and tastes. The demographic profiles of communities also directly influence the amount of disposable income that can be contributed to the arts as well as the amount of direct income that is likely to be derived. It captures the power of taste and communal standards for beauty.

5. Space and Time: Space and time are dimensions that help us understand the influence that the arts have over the centuries and across traditional geographic boundaries. Accounting for time as a multiplier allows us to think about how the arts from past millennia remain relevant today, as well as how today's artistic production might influence future generations. This multiplier also indicates variability in the time taken for different impacts to flow through the system; not all impacts occur at the same speed, and, in some circumstances, it may take lifetimes for a change to register. Space helps us think about how particularly rich forms of artistic expression, while produced locally, can with surprising impact migrate globally.

To sum up, the system map is a conceptual diagram of how variables relevant to the topic of *How Art Works* "talk" to one another. It is a picture of the complexity inherent in discussions of art's impact and it suggests a set of hypotheses about the relationships between arts engagement and the arts' impacts on individuals and their communities. The map offers a platform for mounting a research agenda to test the strength of these relationships and their underlying hypotheses.

In the next two sections, we outline measurement implications of the *How Art Works* system map. Section Three discusses in-depth definitions of key variables and how they might be made operational. Section Four presents the National Endowment for the Arts' five-year research agenda in light of the map and measurement model.

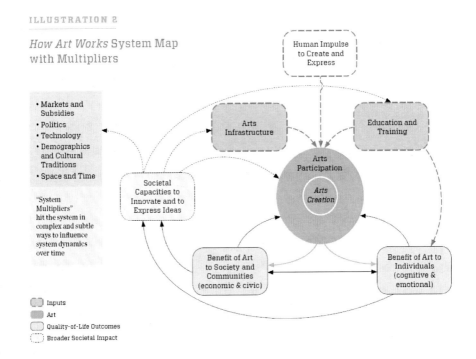

ILLUSTRATION 2

How Art Works System Map with Multipliers

SECTION THREE: DISSECTING THE MAP FOR THE PURPOSE OF MEASUREMENT

Overview

Compellingly specified variables will prove essential if we are to test the hypotheses embedded in the *How Art Works* system map. Any research, regardless of caliber and scale, can be challenged by the argument that variables are mischaracterized. And the outcomes of arts engagement in particular involve many difficult-to-measure concepts. In effect, each node in the system map needs to be further defined and operationalized (i.e., defined in terms of properties that can be independently measured) to support a robust research agenda.

This section of the chapter constructs key variables that can populate the nodes on the system map. The choice of variables in each construct will determine which steps are needed to establish a comprehensive measurement model for the system.

ILLUSTRATION 3

How Art Works Expanded System Map

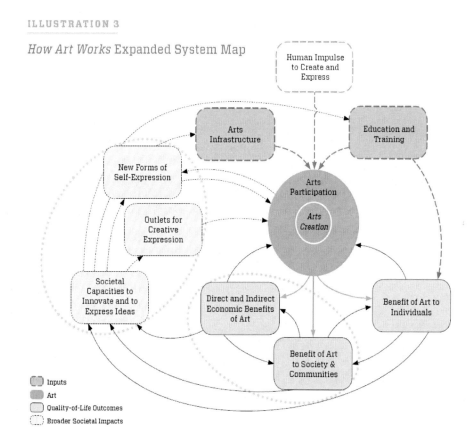

Each construct is illustrated as a sample "multi-level measurement structure" for the node under review. The structures draw from existing research in the field, as well as from multiple interviews, webinars, and convenings.[7] Finally, these constructs are incomplete; in most cases, fuller elaboration and detailed development of subordinate variables are necessary. Gaps are denoted with "place-holder" labels.

But first, for the purpose of understanding the variables in greater detail, we consulted an expanded version of the system map (see Illustration 3). In this version, we separate the benefits to a community from the economic benefits (thus reflecting the substantial body of research existing in each domain), and we isolate the societal benefits of "new forms of self-expression" and "outlets for creative expression" from the larger societal capacity "to innovate and to express ideas."

This section focuses specifically on the nodes of *Inputs, Art,* and *Quality-of-Life Outcomes.* The broad societal impact nodes, in our view, should be explored only once a stronger research program is in place for the primary (quality-of-life) effects. Nevertheless, we acknowledge the broad societal impacts as important outcomes.

We are not specifying the variable *Human Impulse to Express and Create,* since in the system map it represents the fundamental spark of human creativity.

Accordingly, we discuss the following nodes reflected in the expanded system map:

- Input variables
  - Arts Infrastructure
  - Education and Training
- Intervening variables
  - Arts Creation
  - Arts Participation
- Quality-of-life outcomes
  - Direct and Indirect Economic Benefits of Art
  - Benefit of Art to Individuals
  - Benefit of Art to Society and Communities
- Broader societal impact
  - Societal Capacities to Innovate and to Express Ideas

Initial Construct of Input Variables

Arts Infrastructure

Initial Definition
Arts Infrastructure refers to the institutions, places, spaces, and formal and informal social support systems that facilitate the creation and consumption of art.

Issues to Explore in Variable Creation
To create variables using this definition, it is necessary at minimum to determine:

1. How broadly to define infrastructure;
2. How to capture all types of non-financial support; and
3. Whether to include place-based distinctions.

The categories listed in the sample measurement structure below cover a wide range of infrastructure types, including physical spaces, organizations, associations, and other financial and non-financial support.

In the sample measurement structure, "Arts Venues" is divided into "Core" and "Non-Core" venues to indicate the possible relevance of *both* spaces that are primarily used for art-based work *and* those which have another primary function but may include artistic programming (e.g., "core" would include museums and theaters devoted to musical or theatrical performance while "non-core" would include schools and parks, which can serve as venues for exhibits or performances, but which have primary functions other than being arts venues). "Possible Type Elaboration" placeholders indicate that further refinement of the variable is needed for each type of infrastructure.

The sample measurement structure also includes an "Other Infrastructure" placeholder, which reflects the possibility of including additional infrastructure types such as new technology-enabled platforms (e.g., social-network fundraising) and other types of support structures (e.g., health insurance and other benefits, equipment and materials, and access to information).

ILLUSTRATION 4

Example of *Arts Infrastructure* as a Multi-Level Measurement Structure

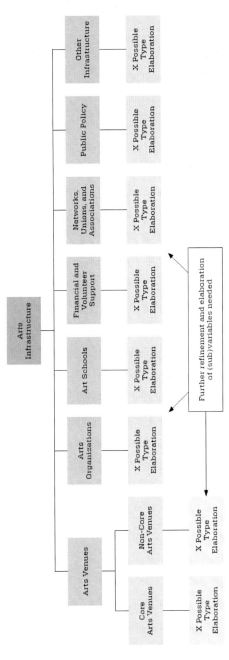

Some Definitional Questions and Methodological Challenges

- There may be insufficient data available.
- Type of infrastructure may be more important than quantity.
- The impact of increasing infrastructure density may not be linear (e.g., more may not always be better).
- Additional political or community context may matter in mediating the importance of arts infrastructure.
- It is critical to ensure that arts infrastructure variables are distinct from variables of Economic Benefits of Art, since they could be defined in ways that overlap; treatment of labor will be of particular importance.

ILLUSTRATION 5

Example of *Education and Training* as a Multi-Level Measurement Structure

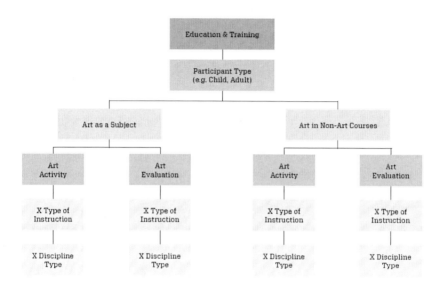

Some definitional questions and methodological challenges

- There may be insufficient data available, particularly with respect to informal arts education (e.g. through the Internet, learning about the arts at home, and self-taught arts).
- There is an issue of confoundedness with education, as some education that is not directly arts-related closely influences arts appreciation (e.g., knowledge of mythology).
- Additional dimensions could focus on quality, frequency, specific exposure (e.g., ability to play a musical instrument), and/or access.
- Quality of arts education may be difficult to measure without the creation and distribution of cost-effective, replicable tools for assessing student and teacher learning in the arts across a variety of arts disciplines.
- It is difficult to capture arts exposure in non-arts classes.
- As with other education, there may be a threshold effect (e.g., each year of participation is not equivalent in terms of outcomes) regarding arts content.
- Educational impact may depend on learning styles of students (e.g., there may be a large impact on some students but a small effect overall).
- This sample measurement structure does not account for the infrastructure variables of U.S. public and private school systems, inclusive of state departments of education, school districts, schools, and public and private

two-year and four-year colleges, for example. The unique definitional issues and methodological challenges that apply to data-collection within these systems will further complicate measurement of Education and Training within the How Art Works system.

For additional examples of how *Arts Infrastructure* variables might be defined, please see a selection of relevant studies listed in the corresponding section of Appendix A.

Education and Training

Initial Definition

Education and Training refers to the standards, best practices, knowledge models, and skills that help inform artistic expression on the one hand, and consumption of art on the other. *Education and Training* spans the spectrum of formal and informal instruction, from YouTube and street jam sessions, to K-12 and adult arts education, to apprenticeship and conservatory training.

Issues to Explore in Variable Creation

To create variables using this definition, it is necessary at minimum to determine:

1. Whether and how to differentiate between youth and adult education;
2. How broadly to define education;
3. How to incorporate informal education;
4. Whether to capture some measure of quality or intensity; and
5. Whether and how to include break-downs by disciplines.

For example, the categories listed in the sample measurement structure (Illustration 5) begin with the differentiation between youth and adult participant types, since there is considerable focus in the arts literature on childhood arts education in particular. The sample measurement model then distinguishes between education where art is the explicit subject and classes where art is not the primary focus but is nonetheless an important component (e.g., a language class that includes literature). These variables are further differentiated by whether the educational experience is focused on activity (such as arts production) or evaluation (such as arts appreciation or criticism).

The sample model also includes "Type of Instruction" placeholders to indicate the potential relevance of education delivery method, such as conservatory learning or online arts education. Finally, the sample model includes placeholders for arts disciplines.

For additional examples of how *Education and Training* variables might be defined, please see a selection of relevant studies listed in the corresponding section of Appendix A.

Initial Construct of Intervening Variables

Arts Creation

Initial Definition

The essential agents of *Arts Creation* are the artists, a broadly and inclusively defined group that includes humans who express themselves—within the confines of a set of known or emerging practices and precedence—with the intention of communicating richly to others.

Issues to Explore in Variable Creation

To create variables with this definition, it is necessary at minimum to determine:

1. Which categories of production count for the purpose of determining who is an artist;
2. How to capture amateur artists / art hobbyists;
3. Whether there should be a minimum time regularly spent on artistic production to qualify as an artist; and
4. Whether any other parameters should be included.

The artist categories listed in the sample measurement structure (Illustration 6) come from the occupational categories derived from U.S. Census data and used by the NEA's *Artist in the Workforce* report series. The measurement structure has been expanded to include those who do not earn a living from the production of art. It also includes a placeholder for a time threshold, since it may be preferable to require a weekly or monthly minimum time spent on artistic production to qualify as an artist.

Finally, the sample measurement structure includes an "Other" category placeholder. This "Other" category is meant to capture the possibility of a more expansive definition of arts production that does not fit into the occupational categories currently used.

For additional examples of how *Artist* variables might be defined, please see a selection of relevant studies listed in the corresponding section of Appendix A.

Arts Participation

Initial Definition

Arts Participation is the act of producing, interpreting, curating, and experiencing art. It includes artistic acts (e.g., creating an artifact or directing an arts performance) and the consumption of those outputs.

ILLUSTRATION 6

Example of *Arts Creation* as a Multi-Level Measurement Structure

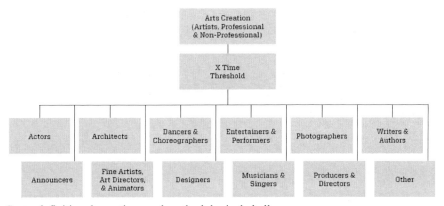

Some definitional questions and methodological challenges

- There may be insufficient data available with respect to non-professional artists. (For instance, there are issues with measuring artistic employment as a secondary occupation, using U.S. Census Bureau methodology.)
- The existing categories might not capture some emergent forms of art production.
- It should be determined whether individuals can define themselves as artists, or whether this variable should be externally defined.
- It is important to ensure that *Arts Creation* variables are sufficiently distinct from variables of Arts Participation, *Economic Benefits of Art*, and *Societal Capacities to Innovate and to Express Ideas*, since they could be defined in ways that overlap unproductively.

Issues to Explore in Variable Creation

To create a variable using this definition, it is necessary at minimum to determine:

1. Which categories of participation to use as a starting point for types of activities covered;
2. How widely to define participation; and
3. Whether to break down participation by hours spent or by another measure (e.g., frequency of discrete activities).

The high-level participation categories in the sample model (Illustration 7) are drawn directly from the definition, while the more detailed categories come primarily from the NEA's Survey of Public Participation in the Arts.

Time spent is included to delineate level of participation, although intensity might be measured instead as the number of times an activity is performed. The "Other" category placeholder indicates the possibility of more expansive definitions of arts experience. The "Possible Type Elaboration" placeholder signifies that multiple types of arts interpretation and curation may be relevant.

For additional examples of how *Arts Participation* variables might be defined, please see a selection of relevant studies listed in the corresponding section of Appendix A.

Initial Construct of First-Order Outcome Variables

Direct and Indirect Economic Benefits of Art

Initial Definition

This node refers to both the direct income derived from the arts (e.g., the price paid for an arts experience or artifact) and the indirect financial returns of the arts (e.g., spending on food, lodgings, and travel that might be associated with going to an arts event). In this context, "benefit" is a neutral word. There can be positive benefit—an artist makes a reasonable income— and there can be negative benefit, such as when an artist cannot support herself because of small or diminishing economic returns, or when someone instead of the artist profits from the artwork at a disproportionate level.

Issues to Explore in Variable Creation

To create variables using this definition, it is necessary at minimum to determine:

1. How to define direct and indirect benefits;
2. How in particular to capture indirect benefits; and
3. Which industries and occupations to include.

The categories listed in the sample measurement structure (Illustration 8) begin with the distinction of direct and indirect benefits. This distinction reflects the strength of connection to arts activity. For example, rental income from an artist's studio or a theater space is a direct effect, while rental income from an arts-district restaurant is indirect.

From this distinction we have derived broad categories of effects, using "income" to denote personal financial benefit and "revenue" to describe dollars flowing to companies and organizations. The difference is somewhat artificial, since most income is paid via salaries, but it is necessary to isolate wage growth from business expansion. Many other forms of economic value occur in both direct and indirect forms, including tax benefits that are derived from nearly every source of direct and indirect value. Similarly, job creation is a direct effect if a staff position is created at a gallery or music venue, but an indirect effect if a restaurant adds staff to accommodate crowds.

There may be multiple degrees of indirectness. For example, hospitality industry effects are a first order of indirect effects (e.g., restaurants and hotels serve visitors to arts destinations). But it may be that industries not engaged in the arts, but which frequently make use of personnel with arts training, relocate to arts-intensive communities to take advantage of a skilled labor pool. Marketing and design firms, advertising agencies, and software companies produce non-arts products but can make use of staff with arts training. This possibility is flagged by the construct "Local Job Creation." Any final measure will require a determination of how inclusive we want to be in capturing indirect effects.

There may also be other components in the final creation of any economic-benefit-of-arts variable. For additional examples of how *Economic Benefits of Art* variables might be defined, please see a selection of relevant studies listed in the corresponding section of Appendix A. Further research could also draw from broader economics and community development literatures.

Benefit of Art to Individuals

Initial Definition

Benefit of Art to Individuals refers to the cognitive, emotional, behavioral, and physiological effects that arts participation can produce in individuals, including transformations in thinking, social skills, and character development over time.

Issues to Explore in Variable Creation

To create a variable using this definition, it is necessary at minimum to determine:

1. What broad categories of individual impact to include;
2. How to measure elements such as aesthetic sensibility, spirituality, and disposition; and
3. Whether to differentiate between the impact on children and adults.

In current literature on the arts' impacts, multiple models seek to identify benefits to individuals. The sample measurement model (Illustration 9) identifies only a few of the potential variables for illustrative purposes. Most of the existing models have significant overlaps and/or slight variations of core concepts. Empirical studies will be needed to determine which factors are most measurable and hold unique variance.

ILLUSTRATION 7

Example of *Arts Participation* as a Multi-Level Measurement Structure

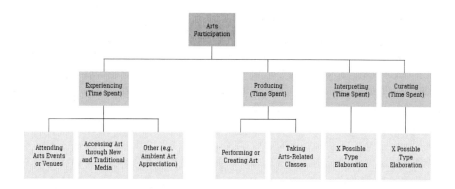

How Art Works 29

- Some definitional questions and methodological challenges.
- There may be insufficient data available, particularly with respect to elements such as "ambient" art enjoyment.
- There is a need to determine how broadly to define art (e.g., whether or not an audience is needed, whether or not there is an aesthetic standard, who defines what is art, and whether creative intention distinguishes art from personal expression).
- It is difficult to capture emergent art forms (i.e., activities that may not yet recognized as art).
- Context matters in mediating the arts experience.
- Different types of participation may matter more for different individuals or populations.
- There is a need to avoid the fallacy of treatment (e.g., that all forms of arts participation produce the same effects).[8]
- There is a need to avoid the fallacy of linearity (e.g., the assumption that more arts participation leads to greater effect).[9]

This sample measurement structure identifies a series of personal characteristics or cognitive states that are frequently cited as elements of a high-quality life. We have focused primarily on internal and social qualities rather than material elements of life-quality, reflecting our view that an arts-sensitive definition of life-quality will be more internal than external. The elements that compose benefit to individuals are not only largely internal; they address a series of psychological constructs that have not been well-established as discrete concepts. Consequently, a key requirement of early research will be developing validation for the variables that are selected.

For additional examples of how a *Benefit of Art to Individuals* variable might be defined, please see a selection of relevant studies listed in the corresponding section of Appendix A. Further research could also draw from broader cognitive science, child development, social psychology, and quality-of-life literatures.

Benefit of Art to Society and Communities

Initial Definition
Benefit of Art to Society and Communities refers to the role that art plays as an agent of cultural vitality, a contributor to sense of place and sense of belonging, a vehicle for transfer of values and ideals, and a promoter of political dialogue.[14]

ILLUSTRATION 8

Example of *Direct and Indirect Economic Benefits of Art* as a Multi-Level Measurement Structure

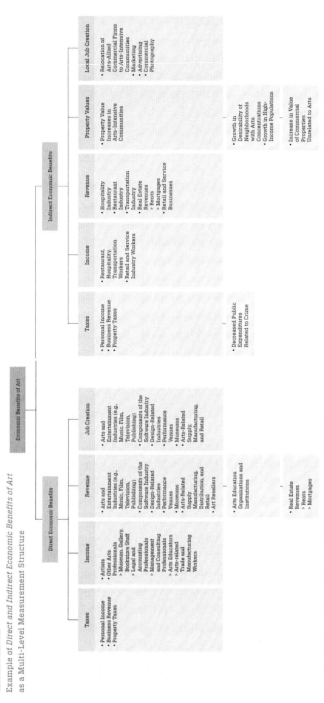

Some Definitional Questions and Methodological Challenges.

- There may be insufficient data available, particularly with respect to indirect benefits.
- Measuring "money" has some distinct and significant challenges. For instance, it is challenging to separate the flow of new money from the redistribution of money within a community (such as a city). Determining whether increased arts participation

is inducing new demand (thus, new money) or is the reallocation of existing demand (less money spent on alternatives so more can be spent on participation) requires sophisticated research techniques and controls.

- It is important to ensure that economic benefit variables are distinct from variables of *Arts Infrastructure* and *Benefit of Art to Society and Communities,* since they could be defined in ways that overlap. For instance, should individual donations to a museum from people living outside the area be considered economic development, even though those donations may go to support the construction of new buildings?
- It is difficult to capture time lag effects in the creation of economic value, particularly in terms of indirect benefits. What are the long term, residual benefits of arts-inspired urban development? And, once new businesses and new residents have moved in and are established, how much of current economic activity can be rightly attributed back to the original development?
- Impact may depend on the type of art and arts participation.
- It will be difficult to determine whether the arts' impact is unique.
- Arts economics studies have traditionally over-focused on metropolitan areas.10
- There is a need to define which industries get counted, as part of the economic value of the arts, within federal statistical systems.

ILLUSTRATION 9

Example of *Benefit of Art to Individuals* as a Multi-Level Measurement Structure

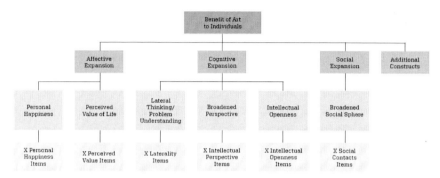

Some definitional questions and methodological challenges.

- There may be insufficient data available, particularly by way of longitudinal assessments of the impacts of art on neurological and motor skill development, creative processes, socialization, critical thinking skills, and illness and disability.[11]
- Impact may depend on type of art and type and frequency of arts participation.
- It may difficult to capture the diffuse and "shallow" effects of a limited but meaningful engagement with art.
- There is a distributional issue, in that a smaller number of people may be very engaged and affected, while a large number may be less affected.
- Some impacts may be more relevant for particular subgroups (e.g., young people).
- Individual responses to art are subjective (e.g., one person may be greatly moved while another remains unmoved).
- It may be difficult to disentangle impacts from other activities in a person's life.
- Consequences can be too removed in space and time for reliable and efficient measurements of cause and effect.
- Impact of arts exposure is influenced by, among other factors, context, relevance, and psychological state.[12]
- There is a need to avoid the fallacy of homogeneity (e.g., that the arts will have the same effects on different types of participants).[13]
- It may be difficult to capture time lag effects.
- It would be ideal to capture the art's benefits relative to exposure to other activities.

ILLUSTRATION 10

Example of *Benefit of Art to Society and Communities* as a Multi-Level Measurement Structure

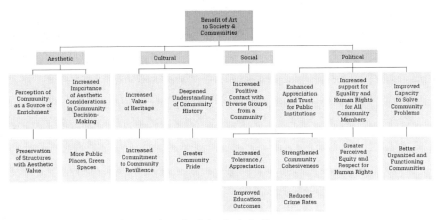

Some definitional questions and methodological challenges.

- There may be insufficient data available, particularly with respect to broad livability elements.
- It may be difficult to determine whether art's impact is unique, particularly given the general social benefit associated with activities that bring people together.[15]
- It may be difficult to capture time lag effects.
- There is a need to differentiate elements from indicators of Arts Infrastructure (e.g., arts volunteers, or outdoor venues where arts performances can occur).
- The "social" column of this structure may overlap with the "cognitive expansion" and "social expansion" columns of the Benefit of Art to Individuals structure.
- There is a need to avoid the fallacy of homogeneity (e.g., that the arts will have the same effects in different types of communities).[16]
- Studies have traditionally over-focused on metropolitan areas.[17]
- It may be important to assess relative effects compared to other spending.[18]
- Impact may depend on the type of art and type of arts participation.
- More diverse communities may be a source of creativity or the result of creative activities.[19]
- It would be ideal to have longitudinal data.[20]

Issues to Explore in Variable Creation

To create variables using this definition, it is necessary at minimum to determine:

1. What elements to include in community benefits;
2. How to define a community; and
3. How to capture heightened social interaction.

The categories listed in the sample measurement structure (Illustration 10) draw from the range of existing constructs hypothesizing benefits of the arts to communities. Some of these indicators can be assessed via community-level variables such as crime rates or educational outcomes. Others—such as cultural and political benefits—must be distinguished from individual-level outcomes so that they are distinct from variables in the *Benefit of Art to Individuals* node.

(In the system map, outcome variables are portrayed as distinct from one another. While this choice has value for comprehending the key elements of the system, some of the map's components may, in practice, be tough to differentiate. Economic and community benefits, for example, interact in complex ways that challenge simple isolation. Therefore, it is worth acknowledging here that the system map depicts components as more distinct than they are when observed in detail.)

The measurement model posits four broad value dimensions of the arts for communities:

1. Communities develop a shared aesthetic appreciation for the character of their place, which assists community decision-making by providing a common frame of aesthetic value;
2. Communities value the shared heritage of their citizenry and value the complex interrelationships among groups of all types;
3. Communities facilitate interaction among people of diverse experiences; and
4. Community members often work cooperatively to solve problems, moved in part by a desire to maintain and improve the aesthetic, cultural, and social value of their shared space.

The system map hypothesizes that arts engagement enhances these qualities.

For additional examples of how a *Benefit of Art to Society and Communities* variable might be defined, please see the relevant studies listed in the corresponding section of Appendix A. Further research could also draw from the broader community development and political science literatures.

Initial Construct of Second-Order Outcome Variable: A Work in Progress

Societal Capacities to Innovate and to Express Ideas

Initial Definition
Societal Capacities to Innovate and to Express Ideas refers to the capacities of community members to "develop, design, or create new applications, ideas, relationships, systems, or products"—individually and collectively.[21]

Issues to Explore in Variable Creation
Societal Capacities to Innovate and to Express Ideas is the least developed of the nodes in the *How Art Works* system map. The experts we assembled agreed on the need for a construct that represents creative energy at a community or societal level. They suggested that variations in a society's capacity to innovate and to express seem observable, and that a higher-order construct might capture this insight. They also held to the belief that the development of the capacity to express is linked with and contributes to a fundamental freedom: our right to express ourselves. This freedom requires certain individual- and community-level attitudes that are facilitated by the arts—for example, the courage to express oneself and a tolerance and even an appetite for new ideas, forms, and outlets for creative expression. As with many abstract constructs, however, arriving at a uniform definition proved difficult. In the course of our work we found that other researchers also have attempted to define and operationalize this capacity, but in our view none has succeeded completely, and there is currently no consensus in the field.[22] Thus, further exploration of the concept remains a future assignment.

Despite definitional issues, there was broad agreement that this capacity is distinct from "generativity" (e.g., revenue earned from sales of a creative product). Therefore, this node currently reflects the potential for creative action, not actual expression (which is found in the attendant nodes *Outlets for Creative Expression* and *New Forms of Self-Expression*) or actual production of economic value (which is covered by the *Direct and Indirect Economic Benefits of Art* node).

Acknowledging this uncertainty, we have chosen not to provide a multilevel measurement structure for *Societal Capacities to Innovate and to Express Ideas,* though perhaps others will explore doing so by leveraging what is known about creative thinking throughout human history. A plausible resource is Steven Johnson's book *Where Good Ideas Come From,* in which the author examines environments that foster the development of "good" ideas that push our careers, our lives, our society, and our culture forward, drawing on subjects as disparate as neurobiology and popular culture. (Johnson identifies population density, access to information, opportunity for nurturing slow hunches, serendipity, acceptance of error, opportunity for exaptation, and presence of layered platforms as elements of innovative environments.) Johnson's ideas express much within the core of notion of *Societal Capacities to Innovate and to Express,* although his work more directly addresses personal creativity rather than a community concept. Nevertheless, Johnson's ideas may offer a reasonable starting point for further efforts to define a social construct of this node and to create a measurement structure for it.

SECTION FOUR: PLOTTING A RESEARCH AGENDA ON THE MAP

Overview and Key Assumptions

So far, we have closely examined one potential model of how art works. We have reviewed inputs to the model, we have placed arts participation (inclusive of arts creation) at the model's center, and we have described a series of first-order outcomes reflecting quality of life for individuals and communities. Further downstream, we have theorized about second-order, "broader societal impacts" that involve capacities for creativity, innovation, and self-expression beyond the arts.

In the preceding chapter, we unpacked the variables that make up the central nodes of our system map: variables related to arts infrastructure and education/ training; to arts participation; and to individual and community-level benefits. Our aim now is to determine which parts of the system map align with the NEA's current research priorities, and how the map can guide the agency's future research directions.

This exercise is not purely speculative. In the Arts Endowment's strategic plan for fiscal years 2012–2016, the agency pledged to develop a five-year Research Agenda with annual milestones. The NEA's Office of Research and Analysis (ORA) consequently has drafted a framework for establishing research priorities on a yearly basis. This framework aligns with the NEA's strategic goal to *Promote Public Knowledge and Understanding about the*

Contributions of the Arts so that, as a direct outcome, *Evidence of the Value and Impact of the Arts is Expanded and Promoted.*

The framework for the NEA's Research Agenda hinges, therefore, on an understanding of two key terms as they pertain to evidence about the arts: "value" and "impact." ORA distinguishes between these terms in the following manner.

Evidence of the arts' value: Descriptive information, primarily statistical, that measures or clarifies factors, characteristics, and conditions of the U.S. arts ecosystem—specifically as they relate to four components:

- Arts Participants and Arts Learners
- Artists and Arts Workers
- Arts Organizations and Arts Industries
- Arts Funders and Arts Volunteers

Evidence of the arts' impact: Quantitative and/or qualitative research data that measure or clarify the benefits of the arts to other domains of American life, including:

- Health and Well-Being
- Cognitive Capacity, Learning, and Creativity
- Community Livability
- Economic Prosperity

As another dimension of the NEA's Research Agenda framework, ORA has identified three overarching goals to guide the unit's annual priority-setting process for research project selection. These goals are:

1. Identify and cultivate new and existing data sources in the arts.
2. Investigate the value of the U.S. arts ecosystem and the impact of the arts on other domains of American life.
3. Elevate the public profile of arts-related research.[23]

These goals are not mutually exclusive. For example, one can imagine a brand-new data source emerging as a byproduct of a study that seeks to explore a particular variable of the U.S. arts ecosystem—just as one inadvertently may "elevate the public profile of arts-related research" through creation of a new dataset. The important point, however, is that ORA has established key objectives for these goals as part of its Research Agenda framework, which will guide ORA's annual priority-setting process.

Collectively, the goals can be viewed as a self-reinforcing feedback loop. High-quality, relevant data sources are a prerequisite for meaningful research to investigate arts topics. New datasets will build capacity among researchers in the field while inspiring scholars from other disciplines to participate in arts-related research. And findings from studies about the arts' value and impact will be distributed widely, to broaden and deepen public engagement with arts-related research questions.

Finding Previous NEA Research on the Map

Now we return to the system map (Illustration 1) from earlier in the document.

Even a cursory review of a list of research publications that the NEA has issued over the past few decades—see arts.gov/research—will reveal that much of the agency's research efforts to date have focused on measuring key variables within the system's "inputs" (*Arts Infrastructure* or *Education and Training*) or within the *Arts Participation* node (inclusive of *Arts Creation*). NEA research also has explored the relationships—indicated on the map by arrows—between the inputs and the central node.

Examples of past NEA research publications that have explored variables of *Arts Infrastructure* are plentiful. They include studies of artists and arts workers, but also arts organizations, arts funders, and even the arts volunteer sector. There are fewer examples of NEA studies focusing on *Education and Training,* though some notable publications have examined trends in exposure to arts education. More common are NEA studies reporting data about *Arts Participation* and *Arts Creation.* These reports stem from the NEA's Survey of Public Participation in the Arts (SPPA), a large, cross-sectional survey of the nation's adults that the U.S. Census Bureau has conducted periodically since 1982.

As noted, there even have been NEA studies that describe the relationship of *Arts Infrastructure* and/ or *Education and Training* to *Arts Participation.* Examples include research publications about the comparative role of venues (e.g., formal or non-formal) to arts-going, and studies about the relationship of literacy skills to the frequency of reading literary works. But perhaps the most conspicuous of these types of studies are reports establishing arts education as a significant predictor of arts participation later in life.

Let's move to the first-order outcomes of arts participation, shown at the bottom of the system map. Historically, the proportion of NEA research devoted to these two distinct but clearly interrelated nodes has been slim indeed.

To be sure, recent years have seen growth in this area, via NEA reports on the links between arts participation and civic engagement (which may be regarded as research on the *Benefit of Art to Society and Communities*), or via NEA research on the positive academic and social outcomes associated with arts engagement among at-risk youth (which may be regarded as research on the *Benefit of Art to Individuals*). Still, there is limited NEA research available about causal inferences that might be drawn from those relationships.

Now see Section Three, Illustration 3, for an "expanded" system map of *How Art Works*. In this depiction, there is an additional first-order outcome of arts participation—namely, the *Direct and Indirect Economic Benefits of Art*. (These benefits fall within the *Benefit of Art to Society and Communities* node in the simpler version of the map.) The NEA has a strong track record of reporting direct economic benefits from the arts. This research typically has been based on reports from the U.S. Bureau of Economic Analysis, Department of Commerce, that show the arts' contribution to Gross Domestic Product for a limited range of industries. As will be seen presently, this reporting capacity could improve substantially in the next few years, as a result of the NEA's Research Agenda.

Stepping back and viewing the system map as a whole, we perceive a research gap associated with the nodes and relationships on the left side of the map: *Societal Capacities to Innovate and to Express Ideas,* and, in the expanded version of the map, *New Forms of Self-Expression* and *Outlets for Creative Expression.*

This deficit is not surprising. As stated earlier in the document, these "second-order" outcomes still require clearer definitions of terms and differentiation of key variables. For researchers, these nodes are signposts. They mark a vast unsettled terrain—a "Wild West" that will yield to only the most intrepid explorers. And yet, over the long term, it ultimately may hold the most promise and profit for those seeking to measure arts-related impacts.

From System Map to Road Map

Although the majority of the NEA's past research has focused on the input variables, intervening variables, and first-order outcomes—as shown on the system map—it is again worth noting that much remains to be done in improving our measurement capacity for these nodes and their relationships. As shown in Section Three, each of these nodes suggests a "multi-level

40 National Endowment for the Arts

measurement structure" with attendant "definitional questions and methodological challenges."

Because of sizeable advances in clarifying these issues over the last several years, moreover, the rewards of short- and near-term investments likely will prove greater and more immediate than for research on second-order outcomes. Accordingly, most of the NEA's research agenda for the next five years will continue to focus on arts infrastructure, education/training, arts participation and creation, and individual and community-level benefits.

The NEA's Office of Research and Analysis has other considerations in making strategic investments. As noted earlier, a primary goal of the office is to *Identify and cultivate new and existing data sources*. Over the next few years, ORA will consolidate large amounts of arts-related data and make them available through user-friendly systems to the public. Although ORA already provides access to raw data and user's manuals for its Survey of Public Participation in the Arts, the office aims to supplement this resource with data and visualizations from other federal, not-for-profit, and industry sources.

Regarding data collection and sharing, the office is uniquely placed to collaborate with federal statistical agencies and with research units elsewhere in the U.S. government. The NEA is a core sponsor agency, along with other federal funders, of the National Academies' Committee on National Statistics. Similarly, in keeping with the NEA's recent history of attracting multiple federal partners for the purpose of serving a broader segment of the population, ORA has forged many research alliances—both formal and informal—with other government agencies. The cultivation of these partnerships will reap many long-term dividends for arts and cultural researchers nationwide.

These investments support the NEA's Research Agenda for FY 2012–2016, given below. They are discussed further in the "Conclusions" section of this chapter.

NEA Research Agenda by Project Title, Summary, and Placement on the System Map

Below is a list of NEA research projects that were identified in FY 2011 or later as priorities for the five-year period starting in FY 2012. At the end of each project summary, the status of the project ("completed," "planned," or "ongoing") is duly noted.

Each summary also includes one or more symbols to indicate the node/s where the project falls on the system map. (AI = *Arts Infrastructure;* E/T = *Education and Training;* AP/AC = *Arts Participation and Arts Creation;* BAI

= *Benefit of Art to Individuals;* BASC = *Benefit of Art to Society and Communities;* DIEBA = *Direct and Indirect Economic Benefits of Art;* and SCIEI = *Societal Capacities to Innovate and to Express Ideas.*) Where multiple symbols are listed for an individual research project, the symbol appearing first in sequence refers to the **primary node** covered by the project.

The project titles are enumerated not necessarily in order of priority or chronology, but mainly so that the accompanying digits can be displayed on the system map illustration to follow. This method enables a visual comparison of the NEA's research priorities by primary node, the results of which comparison might inform project planning in FY 2013 and beyond.

Projects Covering Input Variables

These projects are intended to yield valuable descriptive information primarily about either the Arts Infrastructure or the Education and Training nodes.

1. *Artists and Art Workers in the United States:* Use American Community Survey data to enumerate the nation's artists and to describe their demographic traits, work patterns, and nationwide concentration. Explore links between individual artist occupations and specific industries, and report occupational and industry patterns for workers who obtained arts-related degrees in college. Use a separate data source, the 2010 Quarterly Census of Employment and Wages, to identify state and metropolitan-level concentrations of employment within arts industries. (AI) COMPLETED

2. In-Depth Analysis of Artists in the U.S. Workforce: Provide long-term trend analysis and detailed geographical information (at the state and metro area levels) for 11 distinct artist occupations as captured by American Community Survey data. (AI) PLANNED

3. *How the United States Funds the Arts:* Update the NEA's publication about the nation's decentralized approach to financing arts and cultural activities. This publication will use the most recently available statistics from public and private funders and not-for-profit arts organizations. (AI) ONGOING

4. Federal-State Arts Partnership Data Portal: Explore creation of a publicly accessible web portal that displays data and visualizations about activities undertaken by state arts agencies and regional arts organizations, particularly as a result of the NEA's investments. (AI) ONGOING

5. *Improving Standards and Assessment in Arts Education:* Host and webcast a roundtable event that will provide an opportunity for researchers, educators, and policy-makers to consider the implications of a NEA-commissioned nationwide study of arts assessment tools and practices. (E/T) COMPLETED
6. SPPA 2012 Report on Arts Education: Use the 2012 Survey of Public Participation in the Arts to produce analyses about the frequency and types of arts education that American adults engage in, report for their children, and/or recollect from childhood. (E/T) PLANNED
7. Understanding Arts Education Access by School and School District Characteristics: Analyze raw data from the U.S. Department of Education 's 2010 Fast Response Survey of arts education in public schools, in light of contextual variables from the Department's Common Core of Data. (E/T) PLANNED

Projects Covering Intervening Variables

These projects are intended to yield valuable descriptive information about Arts Participation, inclusive or exclusive of Arts Creation, and how this node relates to the input variables.

8. *An Average Day in the Arts:* Report Americans' daily time-use patterns involving arts participation (e.g., performing arts attendance, museum-going, arts/ crafts activity, writing for personal interest), based on a state-level analysis of the American Time Use Survey for 2006–2010. (AP/AC) COMPLETED
9. SPPA 2012 First Look, Summary Report, and Monograph Series: Release preliminary findings, followed by a comprehensive summary report and a series of monographs based on the 2012 Survey of Public Participation in the Arts, inclusive of data visualizations for the public and user's guides for researchers. Examine trends in arts participation for various disciplines; report baseline data for new disciplines, methods, or forms of participation; and analyze demographic, geographic, and self-reported preferences and behaviors associated with arts participation. (AP/AC) PLANNED
10. ABS Summary Report: Release report, data visualizations, and a data user's guide based on the NEA's 2013 and 2014 Arts Benchmark Survey (ABS), to be conducted by the U.S. Census Bureau. This short-form questionnaire will collect nationally representative data on adult participation in the arts, inclusive of creation, allowing for

capture of U.S. trends in years when the more detailed SPPA is not conducted. (AP/ AC) PLANNED

11. GSS Arts Supplement Report and Monograph/s: Release a summary report, one or more monographs, data visualizations, and a data user's guide based on the General Social Survey (GSS) arts supplement, designed by the NEA to inquire about U.S. adults' motivations for attending (or not attending) arts activities. Data from the supplement will be analyzed in combination with other variables from this large, nationally representative household survey. (AP/AC) PLANNED

12. Innovative Practices in Audience Engagement: Conduct a series of case studies profiling innovative methods of audience engagement, based on a sample of NEA grants, likely in the Arts Presenting category. (AP/AC) PLANNED

Projects Covering First-Order Outcome Variables

These projects are intended to yield valuable descriptive information about the Benefit of Art to Individuals, the Benefit of Art to Society and Communities, and the Direct and Indirect Economic Benefits of Art, and, where possible, how those nodes relate to the input and/ or intervening variables.

13. Audience Impact Survey: Measure how audiences register cognitive or emotional "affect" to live exhibits, performances, or film festivals in a sample of NEA grant projects. (BAI, AP/AC) ONGOING

14. The Arts and Subjective Well-Being: Commission or conduct an analysis of the arts' relationship to subjective well-being, potentially using national data from Gallup's Healthways Index. (BAI) PLANNED

15. NEA-NIH Literature Review and Gap-Analysis: Collaborate with the National Institutes of Health program officers and librarians, along with other members of the NEA's Interagency Task Force on the Arts and Human Development, to conduct a review and gap-analysis of peer-reviewed literature featuring arts interventions at various stages of human development. Results from this analysis are intended to guide future research investments by funding agencies. (BAI) ONGOING

16. NEA-NIH-NAS Public Workshop and Paper Series on the Arts and Aging: Collaborate with three National Institutes of Health entities (the National Institute on Aging, the Office of Behavioral and Social

Sciences Research, and the National Center for Complementary and Alternative Medicine) and the National Academy of Sciences to produce a workshop on the arts' relationship to health and well-being in older adults. The workshop, and five commissioned papers, will identify research gaps and opportunities for further investment by the funding agencies. (BAI) ONGOING

17. NEA-National Intrepid Center of Excellence Research Partnership: Assist and advise in protocol development for a research study to assess clinical outcomes associated with expressive writing therapy as part of a comprehensive care regimen for warriors experiencing traumatic brain injury, post-traumatic stress, and other psychological illnesses. (BAI) ONGOING

18. National Children's Study Arts/Music Supplement: Collaborate with the National Institutes of Health (National Institute of Child Health and Human Development), the Centers for Disease Control and Prevention, and the Environmental Protection Agency to include variables about arts and, specifically, music exposure in early childhood development, for the purpose of long-term analysis of the impact of this variable on cognitive, emotional, health, and educational outcomes in a longitudinal study population. (BAI,BASC) ONGOING

19. *The Arts and Achievement in At-Risk Youth:* Report on an analysis of arts-related variables from four large datasets—three maintained by the U.S. Department of Education and one by the Department of Labor—to understand the relationship between arts engagement and positive academic and social outcomes in children and young adults of low socioeconomic status. (BAI, BASC) COMPLETED

20. Analysis of Arts Participation Among Children and Families: Explore the strength of the relationship between arts participation in children and families and their reported behavioral outcomes over time, based on the Panel Study of Income Dynamics. (BAI, BASC) ONGOING

21. Health Retirement Study Arts Supplement: Design an arts-related module for inclusion in a longitudinal survey of Americans over 50 years old, to investigate health and well-being variables in relation to creativity and arts participation. (BAI, BASC) PLANNED

22. Randomized, Controlled Trial of Arts Education: Conduct a feasibility study for a randomized, controlled trial investigating the long-term effects of an arts education intervention on a metropolitan-area cohort. (BAI,BASC) PLANNED

23. Arts and Livability Indicators: Design, validate, and publish a set of national indicators that can be used to measure outcomes that align with the goals of creative place making projects. Publish a directory of local data sources that can be used to create comparable indicators at the local community level. (BASC) ONGOING

24. American Housing Survey Arts Supplement: Collaborate with the U.S. Department of Housing and Urban Development to explore the design of survey questions—for inclusion on the American Housing Survey—to investigate the role of arts and cultural participation in choosing place of residency, as well as arts/design considerations in home selection and renovation. (BASC) PLANNED

25. Arts and Cultural Production Satellite Account: Work with the Bureau of Economic Analysis, Department of Commerce, to establish a national account of arts and cultural industries, including annual estimates on number of establishments, their employment, compensation, output, and "value added" to Gross Domestic Product. (DIEBA) ONGOING

Projects Covering Second-Order Outcome Variables

These projects are intended to yield valuable descriptive information about the Benefit of Art to Societal Capacities to Innovate and to Express Ideas, and, where possible, how this node relates to the input and/ or intervening variables.

26. *The Arts, New Growth Theory, and Economic Development:* Commission, present, and publish a paper series examining potential applications of endogenous growth theory and other innovative economic models to the study of art's impact. (SCIEI) ONGOING

27. Analysis of Arts Variables in the Rural Establishment Innovation Survey: Examine the potential impact of arts and entertainment options on companies' decisions to locate in a particular community, based on an item proposed by ORA and subsequently included in a U.S. Department of Agriculture survey. (SCIEI) PLANNED

28. Study of Design Patents and Product Innovation: Collaborate with the U.S. Patent and Trademark Office on a research paper exploring the relationship between design and utility patent-holders, with an emphasis on innovative product development. (SCIEI) PLANNED

Projects Covering All Nodes

These projects are intended to build long-term capacity for the field to undertake studies that can enable measurement of any given node and/or its relationship to other nodes. Because the projects do not relate to one node in particular, they do not appear on the system map illustration above.

29. *Research: Art Works:* Adjudicate, recommend for funding, and award grants to support research and analysis to investigate the value of the U.S. arts ecosystem and the impact of the arts on other domains of American life. The NEA will post research findings, methodology, data sources, and where possible, raw data on the agency's website. ONGOING

30. Online Data Repository: Build a data repository with arts-related datasets, visualizations, and research resources for broad public access, including specialized tools for researchers. ONGOING

31. Virtual Research Network: Create or sponsor an online portal and/or listserv that allows arts and cultural researchers to interact and to share working papers, methodological problems and solutions, and data sources, for the purpose of fostering collaborative inquiries about the value and impact of the arts. PLANNED

Analysis

By aligning the Arts Endowment's five-year research priorities with the system map components shown above, the NEA's Office of Research and Analysis (ORA) can achieve a better understanding of how all the items in its portfolio relate to each other conceptually. ORA can track the relative allocation of recent, planned, and current research projects to different nodes on the map of *How Art Works*: the system's inputs, the intervening variables that sit at its center, and its first- and second-order outcomes. Based on results from this ongoing assessment, ORA can take action to fill gaps in its portfolio, or to bring it into balance with emerging needs and realities that affect the system.

An initial review of ORA's research agenda as it fits on the map suggests at least four points for discussion and potential action:

- For volume of research projects per node, *Arts Participation* (inclusive of *Arts Creation*) and *Benefit of Art to Individuals* each claim the largest share. This fact reflects the NEA's programmatic emphasis on the values of creativity, arts engagement, and the arts' relationship to quality of life—but it is also a function of available data sources and opportunities for data collection. Most projects on these nodes, or on the *Arts Infrastructure* and *Education and Training* nodes, are made possible only by historical data collections (e.g., the SPPA) or new or planned surveys (e.g., the National Children's Study).

For example, with *Direct and Indirect Economic Benefits of Art* and *Benefit of Art to Society and Communities,* there is a clear need to build national time-series (preferably longitudinal) data collections including arts variables. This need could be partly met by ORA's project #25, "Arts and Cultural Production Satellite Account," which may produce time-series data on the value added to the U.S. GDP by arts and cultural industries. Availability of such data may fuel additional research projects to populate that node.

- The detailed component variables of the system map—as presented in Section Three of this chapter— warrant further analysis for the purpose of developing a comprehensive measurement model of the arts as a system. Rather than attempt to construct and validate those variables node by node, the NEA's Office of Research and Analysis likely will consult the model throughout the five-year agenda period so that any advances in measurement may be reached in the context of individual research projects. Similarly, the impacts of various "system multipliers" (see Section Two) may be tracked on a periodic basis.

- ORA will need to determine the extent to which it can plan studies within a five-year period to address the nodes of *Outlets for Creative Expression, New Forms of Self-Expression,* and, though technically a catalyst of the system itself, *Human Impulse to Create and Express.* (In the latter category, for example, one envisions research of an anthropological bent, perhaps through textual analysis, case histories, or observational studies that clarify primal links between human communication and creativity.) A reasonable approach might be to lodge these concepts in the broader dialectic of the arts research community, so that new hypotheses, research questions, populations, data sources, and methods might be proposed by groups outside the NEA.

ILLUSTRATION 11

NEA Research Projects for Fiscal Years 2012-2016, Identified by Primary Node on the *How Art Works* System Map

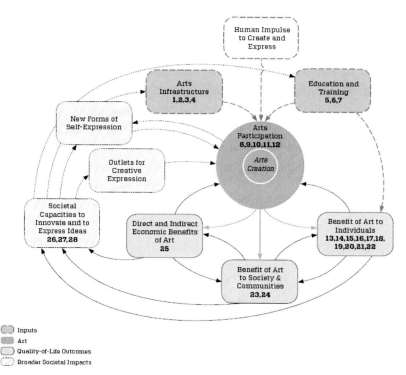

How to read this map

This map is an expanded version of the How Art Works system map, also shown in Illustration 3, but with a difference. Most of the nodes contain numbers that are linked to specific projects on the NEA's five-year research agenda. (See the accompanying "NEA Research Agenda by Project Title, Summary, and Placement on the System Map.") If a number appears on a node, then the project associated with that number falls primarily within the domain of inquiry represented by the node.

- For long-term planning and evaluation of resources, it may be worth establishing a hierarchy among the projects represented on the arrows, by distinguishing among projects that attempt to posit or test correlations between the nodes, and those which seek to establish cause-and-effect relationships, especially since the latter types of projects are traditionally scarce within the arts research field.

CONCLUSION

The theory-based system map and measurement model in this chapter will lead to greater reflection and more deliberate planning within the NEA's Office of Research and Analysis. Beyond this outcome, the chapter invites researchers, practitioners, and policy-makers in the arts and in other sectors to examine the constructs and definitions used, and to question the choices made in including or excluding certain variables. The map may even generate alternative hypotheses or measurement models that can be tested alongside those in the chapter. The net results of such inquiries would strengthen the field of arts research as a whole, and, secondarily, would inform policy and practice with more relevant and meaningful data.

For now, the system map offers a platform not only for the NEA's own research and measurement activity, but also for other public and private stakeholders who may see fit to tackle one or more of the definitional or methodological challenges raised by the chapter.

It is unlikely that any single agency or organization can set into motion all the processes needed to elaborate the system map's variables and their relationships for the purpose of measurement. But if something like a consensus might emerge among arts researchers, for understanding at least a portion of the map, then perhaps more fruitful collaborations would arise. There would be more targeted research investments, reducing duplicative effort and avoiding the dissonance that sometimes occurs in the field when one seeks to describe the arts' impacts, let alone measure them.

A side benefit of producing this chapter was taking stock of the growth and accomplishments of the arts research community over the past few decades. The NEA's Office of Research and Analysis aims to build on that impressive body of knowledge while inspiring a new generation of research into the characteristics and contributions of art in American life. From its perch within the U.S. government, the office is poised to advance this work on two frontiers: by throwing a spotlight on large national datasets that may hold value for arts research; and by establishing strategic ties with other federal agencies.

- *Large national datasets:* The advent of "big data" provides researchers and policy-makers with a means for supplementing, or even supplanting, traditional survey data. Although many of those opportunities involve use of commercial, transactional data, they also reside in government and not-for-profit sectors, through detailed administrative records.

Systematic access to such data is staggering to contemplate, and is attended, in some cases, by unresolved issues of privacy and confidentiality. Also, as noted frequently by Robert Groves, former director of the U.S. Census Bureau and current provost of Georgetown University, there are tradeoffs in quality and cost that must be negotiated, particularly by social scientists who have grown accustomed to working with rigorous data quality standards.[24] Yet one would be short-sighted not to explore these possibilities with respect to information about, say, arts participation. In this respect, the arts may be an ideal domain of inquiry, given the prevalence of creativity and self-expression on technological platforms for which commercial data exist.

Over the period of its research agenda, the NEA's Office of Research and Analysis has committed to make available public datasets and user's guides—along with the results of analyses—for the large, nationally representative surveys it conducts. The office also will house a data repository that will enable researchers to search for arts variables across a wide range of publicly accessible data and to perform basic analyses and visualizations. It is likely that the repository will include the NEA's own grants data, where applicable, as well as links to research papers resulting from NEA research grants. Those awards support projects that seek to mine secondary data sources for evidence of the arts' value and impact.

- *Strategic ties with other federal agencies:* If the NEA is to be successful in promoting public-private partnerships in arts research and in encouraging multidisciplinary research collaborations, then the agency should start close to home. Over the last few years, accordingly, the NEA's Office of Research and Analysis (ORA) has reached out to other federal departments, agencies, offices, and divisions to identify mutual areas of interest and to make available arts-related research information to a broader group of stakeholders than it might have done alone.

  For example, ORA has engaged with the U.S. Census Bureau on two distinct surveys as a supplement to existing data collections. Also regarding data access and availability, ORA has worked with the Bureau of Economic Analysis (Commerce Department) and the Bureau of Labor Statistics (Department of Labor). And the office has teamed formally and informally with the National Science Foundation in projects ranging from inclusion of arts-related questions on a national survey to the public presentation of research about music learning and improved cognitive ability.

Among the office's most significant accomplishments, by way of federal partnerships, is the creation of an Interagency Task Force on the Arts and Human Development, representing 14 federal entities such as the U.S. Department of Health and Human Services, the National Institutes of Health, the Institute of Museum and Library Services, and the U.S. Department of Education. As one of their first projects, Task Force members cosponsored a public workshop with the National Academy of Sciences, whose National Research Council commissioned papers exploring the relationship between the arts and health and well-being in older Americans.

Similarly, the office is taking part in protocol development for the National Children's Study—a joint initiative by NIH and the Centers for Disease Control and Prevention and the Environmental Protection Agency—and protocol development for research to validate arts therapy at the National Intrepid Center of Excellence at the Walter Reed National Military Medical Center. In the future, ORA aims to collaborate with researchers at the U.S. Department of Housing and Urban Development to understand the arts' potential role in a series of metrics for livable communities.

These examples give a taste of the complex resource requirements for a sustainable research program in the arts, one that can make demonstrable progress over the next five years in spurring high-quality proposals to study the arts' value and impact. No map or blueprint can show the way entirely. At best it can function like a jazz musician's score: performance will depend partly on skills of interpretation, and partly on gifted improvisation along the way. Yet, with any luck, some of the concepts and research questions throughout this chapter may in time become "standards," sparking original contributions from a growing ensemble of players. Together, we can bring new talent and resources to answer age-old questions about the arts and their importance to quality of life.

The NEA's Inaugural Research Grants Portfolio

Since the establishment of a research program at the National Endowment for the Arts in 1975, the agency has relied mainly on staff expertise and contractors to conduct studies on the arts. In 2011, for the first time, the NEA's Office of Research and Analysis announced a competitive grants opportunity for research proposals that will mine secondary datasets for information about the arts' value and/or impact. Under *Research: Art Works,* 14 grant awards were made in 2012, totaling nearly $250,000. Below is the list of funded projects. As with the list of FY 2012–2016 Research Agenda projects shown earlier in this section, the FY 2012 *Research: Art Works* project descriptions appear with symbols (in parenthesis) reflecting particular "nodes" on the *How Art Works* system map.

Brown University
PROVIDENCE, RI
To support a study to identify the long-term social and cognitive impacts on children and teenagers who received music training. The research will examine results from a 50-year longitudinal data collection, the New England Family Study, to demonstrate the impacts of music training on teen and adult criminal behavior and other adverse social outcomes (e.g., substance use, low self-esteem), as well as long-term cognitive effects. (BAI, BASC)

Creative Alliance Milwaukee
MILWAUKEE, WI
To support an inventory and analysis of datasets and definitions used to profile creative economies or industries. The results will yield a "core" definition and dataset that national and local policymakers can adopt to understand the relationship of arts and cultural sectors to other creative industries. Also, the project seeks to place creative industries in a broader economic policy context. (SCIEI, DIEBA)

Fordham University
NEW YORK, NY
To support a study of the impact of arts programming on the social skills and mental health outcomes of at-risk youth. Data will be examined from two Florida programs that served youth who had been arrested or had received multiple suspensions from school. By comparing outcomes in youth who participated in arts programs with outcomes in youth who did not, this project

How Art Works 53

will help fulfill a critical knowledge gap that may have consequences for youth intervention programs and greater public policy concerning at-risk populations. (BAI, BASC)

Georgia Tech Research Corporation
ATLANTA, GA

To support a two-phase study investigating: (1) the value of time spent by Americans on arts-related activities, and (2) an analysis of the impacts of arts districts on neighborhood characteristics. The first phase of the study will examine costs of activities such as traveling to and from arts events, based on data from the U.S. Department of Labor's American Time Use Survey and the U.S. Census Bureau's Current Population Survey. A second phase of the study will use a proprietary data-set to analyze the relationship between arts district clustering and the economic value and socioeconomic characteristics of U.S. neighborhoods. (AP/AC, DIEBA, BASC)

Harvard University
CAMBRIDGE, MA

To support a study of causal factors pertaining to the "birth" and "death" rates of arts and cultural institutions. This project will analyze IRS Form 990s from nonprofit arts and cultural institutions in six urban centers to compare survival rates between 1989 and 2009. Among factors that will be explored are: size of organization; funding sources and levels; type of organization; location; and geographic concentration. The resulting knowledge will contribute to public understanding of factors related to the sustainability of a U.S. arts infrastructure. (AI)

National Dance Education Organization
SILVER SPRING, MD

To support a project to identify, analyze, and summarize data that demonstrate the impact of dance education across multiple domains. The researchers will mine the Dance Education Literature and Research descriptive index, a database including 5,000 citations of dance education research from 1926 to the present. This meta-analysis will result in three separate research reports. The reports will describe the value of dance education as a learning modality for creative and critical thinking skills and social and emotional development. (E/T, BAI)

University of Dayton
DAYTON, OH

To support a study of the relationship between arts engagement and quality of life, as reflected by economic well-being and civic engagement patterns. The study will examine data from several waves of the Current Population Survey and its Survey of Public Participation in the Arts supplements in order to explore this relationship. Researchers will use factor analysis and structural equation modeling of survey variables to create constructs of economic well-being and civic engagement; logistic regression will be used to predict the impact of arts engagement on these constructs. Further, by differentiating between "traditional" and "customized" arts participation, the study will add a finer-grained analysis to complement existing research about the arts and civic engagement. (AP/AC, BASC)

University of Georgia
ATHENS, GA

To support a qualitative research analysis to generate a hypothesis about community-built practices to inform policies and programs. The term "community-built" describes a practice whereby artists and designers involve local volunteers in the design, organization, and construction of projects such as playgrounds, mosaic sculptures, murals, community gardens, and amphitheaters. Literature to be analyzed will include press articles, websites, and books written by members of the Community Built Association, founded in 1989. This research will expand knowledge of the arts by defining a new area of study within the fields of art and design. (AP/AC, BASC)

University of Illinois at Chicago
CHICAGO, IL

To support a study to examine the impact of arts exposure and artistic expression on society, including civic engagement and social tolerance. Using behavioral data collected from the General Social Survey—a nationally representative sample of U.S. households— the study will use multivariate analysis to test hypotheses about the impact of arts exposure on society and the impact of artistic expression on individual civil behavior. (BASC)

University of Maryland at College Park
COLLEGE PARK, MD

To support analysis of the cognitive, behavioral, and social outcomes of adolescents who study the arts in comparison with teenagers who do not.

Analysis will be conducted with data from the National Longitudinal Study of Adolescent Health, a multi-year study of American adolescents that tracked participants from adolescence through early adulthood. The arts and non-arts students will be compared in terms of their school engagement, psychological adjustment, delinquency, involvement in risky behaviors, and substance use during adolescence. (BAI, BASC)

University of Texas at Arlington
ARLINGTON, TX
To support a cross-sectional analysis of 30 U.S. cities over three decades to identify neighborhood attributes driving location preferences for artists and artistic businesses. The use of multivariate time-series data and geospatial mapping will enable statistical methods to test a causal relationship between the presence of the arts and neighborhood development. The results could contribute to the development and refinement of social and economic policies that promote positive neighborhood change. (BASC, AT)

University of Texas at Austin
AUSTIN, TX
To support a study to examine current levels of diversity among arts boards and audiences, and identify factors associated with fostering or inhibiting greater board and audience diversity. This study will explore the Urban Institute's National Survey of Nonprofit Governance, a dataset of 476 arts, culture, and humanities organizations, as well as 4,639 nonprofit organizations in other fields of activity, thus allowing for comparative analysis. Arts organizations and their supporters increasingly have expressed a commitment to greater diversity. This study will provide arts organizations, funders, and policymakers with information to help them assess and improve strategies for achieving that goal. (AI, AP/AC)

Vanderbilt University
NASHVILLE, TN
To support an analysis of the relationship between creative practice and subjective well-being in individuals studied by three national surveys. Using data from the Strategic National Arts Alumni Project, the DDB Needham Life Style Survey, and a Teagle Foundation-funded study of students with double-majors, researchers will explore potential correlations between art-making and quality of life. The resulting chapter will offer a theoretical basis for understanding links between creative practice and subjective wellbeing, and it

will test those links empirically. Following this study, cultural policymakers will have a better opportunity to align the arts with public policy about individual and community vitality. (BAI)

Williams College
WILLIAMSTOWN, MA

To support a study that will examine whether a causal link exists between cultural activities and economic prosperity, and which investigates the tendency of arts and cultural organizations to cluster in specific neighborhoods. This study uses two novel methodologies—from other, non-arts sectors—to establish a causal relationship between increases in per-capita arts program expenditures and long-run gains in Gross Domestic Product within urban areas. The resulting evidence, and successful use of the methodologies themselves, will enhance public understanding of the arts' economic impact. (DIEBA)

End Notes for Section 1

[1] System mapping is an analytical technique broadly applied in both the social and physical sciences. It allows analysts to picture complex interactions between large numbers of variables combining to generate single outcomes. The constellation of causal variables is referred to as a "system." The "mapping" is the process of first imagining and then testing how variables interact with one another over time to produce impact. The basis of the method is the recognition that the structure of any system—the many circular, interlocking, sometimes time-delayed relationships among its components—is often just as important in determining its behavior as the individual components themselves.

Recent applications of system mapping have proved instrumental in moving policy conversations forward on topics as difficult as the causes, consequences, and policy options for climate change, or the interactions between consumer confidence and financial market performance, or the interplay between charitable giving and social cohesion. While contributions to the field of system-mapping have been made by many leading scientists and social scientists, the Massachusetts Institute of Technology has perhaps contributed more to the field than any other single institution, according to Monitor Institute, the NEA's primary consultant throughout this process. Monitor's approach in Phase II of this initiative drew heavily from the particular contributions of Jay W. Forrester, Peter Senge, and John Sterman, each with deep ties to MIT.

The primary benefit of system mapping is that it often facilitates a breakthrough understanding of contradictions, trade-offs, and tensions routinely found in environments where a wide variety of causes interact with one another across space and time to produce the results of interest. Given the prevalence of these "puzzles" in the discussion of the benefits of art, and in attempts to link art and quality of life, the method suggested itself as an obvious choice for the *How Art Works* project.

[2] The term "cultural vitality" is defined by Rosario Jackson et al.: "Evidence of creating, disseminating, validating, and supporting arts and culture as a dimension of everyday life in communities," from *Cultural Vitality in Communities,* Washington, DC: The Urban Institute (2006).

[3] It is conceivable that some types of art can lead to negative individual outcomes, either directly (i.e., as a direct result of engagement) or indirectly (e.g., due to tradeoffs in time that occur when an individual engages in a specific type of art versus another activity).

[4] Because communities do not all have the same values, ideals, or political inclinations, art that is seen as beneficial by one community can appear threatening to another. For an empirical analysis of this phenomenon in 71 U.S. cities, see *Not Here, Not Now, Not That! Protest over Art and Culture in America,* by Steven J. Tepper.

[5] *Economic Benefits of Art* to an individual or group can at times be at odds with economic benefits to another individual or group (e.g., rising real estate prices in artistic communities benefit local government and real estate agents but burden low-income residents—including some artists—who no longer can afford to pay rent).

[6] The definition of this term comes from literature on creative capacity , specifically from McGranahan and Wojan's (2007) characterization of "thinking creatively," which is rooted in Richard Florida's concept of a "creative class." McGranahan and Wojan, "The Creative Class: A Key to Rural Growth," *Amber Waves* 5:2 (April 2007):16–21.

[7] A measurement structure for each node can be developed and validated by one or more methods. There are both theory-driven and data-driven techniques available for developing variables. In a theory-driven approach, theories are used to identify the elements of any measurement model. In a data-driven approach, pilot data are collected and the elements of the model are selected based largely on statistical criteria. In general, theory-driven models are more powerful because they provide more opportunities for confirmation and rejection. However, arts engagement theory does not seem established enough to rely solely on a theory-driven approach. Thus, we would suggest that the literature be employed to construct initial measurements, but that final research constructs be determined by statistical means.

[8] See McCarthy et al., *Gifts of the Muse,* Santa Monica, CA: RAND Research in the Arts (2004), citing DiMaggio.

[9] Ibid.

[10] See McCarthy et al. (2004).

[11] This assessment of data gaps comes partly from the 2011 white paper *The Arts and Human Development: Framing A Research Agenda for The Arts, Lifelong Learning, and Individual Well-Being,* by the National Endowment for the Arts and the U.S. Department of Health and Human Services.

[12] See Brown and Novak, "Assessing the Intrinsic Impacts of a Live Performance," WolfBrown (2007).

[13] See McCarthy et al. (2004), citing DiMaggio.

[14] Access and participation in cultural activities can also be viewed as an indicator of fairness and social equity. See Aotearo, "Cultural Indicators for New Zealand," Statistics NZ (2006).

[15] See McCarthy et al. (2004).

[16] See McCarthy et al. (2004), citing DiMaggio.

[17] See McCarthy et al. (2004).

[18] Ibid.

[19] See Stern and Seifert, "Cultivating 'Natural' Cultural Districts," The Reinvestment Fund (2007).

[20] See McCarthy et al. (2004).

58 National Endowment for the Arts

[21] The definition of this term comes from literature on creative capacity, specifically from McGranahan and Wojan's (2007) characterization of "thinking creatively," which they used to elaborate their understanding of "creative class." For the present purpose, it is the concept of creative thinking rather than any specific occupational assignment that is most relevant.

[22] For example, Florida (2003) situates the creative capabilities of a community in individuals whose work creates meaningful new forms and in creative professionals who work in knowledge-intensive industries. For Florida, members of the creative class share common values of creativity, individuality, difference, and merit. A Creativity Index can be measured through elements such as the percentage of the creative class out of a total workforce, amount of high-tech industry, patents per capita and a measure of diversity. In contrast to Florida's work, Hoyman and Faricy (2009) found that human capital predicts economic growth and development, while social capital predicts average wage growth. McGranahan and Wojan (2007) call upon a slight redefinition of creative class in their assessment of creative capacity in rural areas, since Florida's definition maps to virtually all occupations that require a high level of schooling. McGranahan and Wojan instead include occupations that involve "thinking creatively," defined as "developing, designing, or creating new applications, ideas, relationships, systems, or products, including artistic contributions" (p. 5). Markusen et al. (2006) avoid the term "creative class" entirely and focus instead on the presence of cultural industries and occupations: those involved in the production of texts and symbols for a society.

[23] As a unit, the NEA's Office of Research and Analysis has a fourth goal: "Evaluate the administration of NEA programs for impact and effectiveness." These reviews occur as part of an annual performance measurement plan that informs the NEA's Performance and Accountability (PAR) report to the White House Office of Management and Budget, Congress, and the American public. In addition, ORA routinely conducts grants portfolio reviews to inform agency decision-making. The unit also responds to periodic requests, from leadership, to assess the performance of a specific NEA division, program, or initiative.

[24] "Census Chief Robert Groves: We've Got to Stop Counting Like This," *Washington Post*, Aug. 5, 2012

In: Measuring the Arts
Editors: K. O'Connell and D. Myrick

ISBN: 978-1-62618-269-1
© 2013 Nova Science Publishers, Inc.

Chapter 2

HOW ART WORKS: THE NATIONAL ENDOWMENT FOR THE ARTS' FIVE-YEAR RESEARCH AGENDA, WITH A SYSTEM MAP AND MEASUREMENT MODEL, APPENDIX A AND APPENDIX B*

National Endowment for the Arts

APPENDIX A

Below are brief descriptions of relevant studies and datasets for each node in the *How Art Works* system map.

This appendix is not a comprehensive overview of all available work that relates to each concept. Instead, it is meant to supply examples of how such concepts are discussed in the literature and (in some cases) which variables may be used for future research and metrics development. The titles appear in descending chronological order.

The list was compiled by Monitor Institute for the National Endowment for the Arts' Office of Research and Analysis (ORA). The ORA staff wish to thank Aimee Fullman, who conducted a literature review that benefited this project at an early stage.

---

* This is an edited, reformatted and augmented version of a National Endowment for the Arts Report.

INPUTS

Arts Infrastructure

Examples of Relevant Studies

- *"Set in Stone: Building America's New Generation of Arts Facilities, 1994-2008,"* by Joanna Woronkowicz et al. (2012) — Assesses cultural facilities and building projects in the U.S., including community effects.
- *"Still Kicking: Aging Performing Artists in NYC and LA Metro Areas: Information on Artists IV,"* by Joan Jeffri (2011) — Draws from respondent-driven surveys of performing artists, ages 62 and older, in the New York City and Los Angeles metro areas. The report investigates topics such as access to health insurance, work satisfaction, earnings, and other issues confronting senior performing artists.
- *"California's Arts and Cultural Ecology,"* by Ann Markusen, Anne Gadwa, Elisa Barbour, and William Beyers (2011) — Uses a variety of data sets, including the California Cultural Data Project, the American Community Survey, and the Survey of Public Participation in the Arts, to explore the budget sizes, geographic locations, and intrinsic and economic impacts from 11,000 arts and cultural nonprofits in California.
- *"The Annual Report on Philanthropy for the Year 2010,"* by Giving USA (2011) — Captures rates of philanthropic giving, including for arts and culture and the humanities.
- *"Creative Placemaking,"* by Ann Markusen and Anne Gadwa (2010) — Discusses the role local arts and cultural organizations play in community revitalization and economic development. The report presents case studies ranging from the development of an arts district in Cleveland to the transformation of a vacant Buffalo auto plant into artist studios and housing.
- *"Artist Space Development: Making the Case,"* by Maria Rosario Jackson and Florence Kabwasa Green (2007) — Draws on research conducted in seven U.S. cities to explore the development of affordable spaces for artists to live and work; suggests strategies that may be used to advocate for artist spaces; and discusses expected

outcomes of developing artist spaces, such as community economic development.

- *"Cultivating 'Natural' Cultural Districts,"* by M. Stern and S. Seifert (2007) — Describes "natural" cultural districts as opportunities for time-limited, strategic interventions to expand their effectiveness while generating revenue and spillover effects to other parts of the city.
- *"Cultural Vitality in Communities: Interpretation and Indicators,"* by Maria Rosario Jackson et al. (2006) — Provides an assessment of various indicators for the presence of opportunities for cultural participation, cultural participation itself, and support for cultural participation.
- *"Crossover: How Artists Build Careers across Commercial, Non-Profit Work and Community Work,"* by Ann Markusen et al. (2006) — Explores how each sector is organized in Los Angeles and the Bay Area and how artists move between them. Each sector provides different channels and support for artistic development.
- *"Investing in Creativity: A Study of the Support Structure for U.S. Artists,"* by Maria Rosario Jackson et al. (2003) — Uses data from the New York Foundation on the Arts, as well as data surveyed from artists and from case studies, to investigate support for individual artists. The study assesses the political and social climates for supporting artists, demand for artists' work, and training needs and grant opportunities for artists.

Examples of Relevant Datasets[1]

- *Bureau of Labor Statistics' Current Population Survey, Occupational Outlook Handbooks, and Current Employment Statistics* — Provides employment, demographic, wage and worker characteristics data by job classification. As of 2002, the Current Population Survey also includes a supplement on volunteer activities.[2]
- *IRS Tax Statistics* — Data aggregated to zip-code level, with entity numbers, receipts and net income at the Arts, Entertainment and Recreation level. Form 990 data is available for tax-exempt organizations.
- *National Center for Charitable Statistics' (NCCS) Unified Database of Arts Organizations (UDAO)* — Provides a master list of

commercial, nonprofit, and governmental organizations with arts programs.

- *U.S. Census Bureau's County Business Patterns* — Provides sub-national economic data by industry, including number of employees, type of organization and payroll.
- *U.S. Census Bureau's Economic Census* — Provides economic data on performing arts, museum and historical sites, including number of establishments, receipt and employment data.
- *U.S. Census Bureau's Nonemployer Statistics* — Offers sub-national economic data by industry, including number of businesses and total receipts, for businesses that have no paid employees.

Education and Training

Examples of Relevant Studies

- *"The Arts and Achievement in At-Risk Youth: Findings from Four Longitudinal Studies,"* by James Catterall et al. (2012) — Study on the benefits of arts education for at-risk children, using longitudinal data from the Departments of Education and Labor. Includes data on civic engagement, graduation rates and labor market outcomes.
- *"Arts Education in America: What the Declines Mean for Arts Participation,"* by Nick Rabkin and E. C. Hedberg (2011) — This report investigates the relationship between arts education and arts participation, based on the Survey of Public Participation in the Arts for 1982, 1992, 2002, and 2008. The report also examines long-term declines in Americans' reported rates of arts learning.
- *"Fostering Student Engagement Campuswide – Annual Results 2011,"* by National Survey of Student Engagement (2011) — This report is based on responses from 416,000 undergraduate students completing the 2011 NSSE. Results are reported by major, including arts and humanities majors, and it covers topics such as the percentage of students consulting with faculty about career plans; the average time spent studying; and the share of students with concerns about paying for college. Includes demographic characteristics and information about extracurricular activities.
- *"Forks in the Road: The Many Paths of Arts Alumni,"* by Strategic National Arts Alumni Project (2011) — Tracks the careers of artists

with visual and performing arts degrees, including work in an arts-related field, continued arts production, and use of arts training.

- *"Both/And: Understanding the Vital Link Between both the Arts and Career Technical Education in California Schools,"* by J. Landon and Dana Powell Russell (2010) — Explores the interrelationship between policies and infrastructure currently in place within Career Technical Education and Visual and Performing Arts education.
- *"The Nation's Report Card: Arts 2008 Music and Visual Arts,"* by S. Keiper et al. (2009) — Reports the findings of an assessment of the skills of 8th-graders in music and visual arts. Includes an assessment of the frequency of arts instruction.
- *"Artists in the Workforce: 1990-2005,"* by NEA Office of Research and Analysis (2008) — Provides employment, income, demographic and geographic information on 11 artistic occupations assembled from U.S. Census Bureau's decennial data and the American Community Survey.

Examples of Relevant Datasets[4]

- *Bureau of Labor Statistics' American Time Use Survey* — Includes employment classifications and time spent on arts and entertainment activities on a given day. Because of the daily measurement, activities are grouped into broader categories.
- *General Social Survey* — Includes demographic, occupational, educational, income, physical and emotional well-being and membership data as part of broad attitudinal survey. 2002 module included more arts-specific data. Membership in art or literary groups, volunteer in arts or culture, arts philanthropy, visit to museum or gallery, visit to internet art sites, performance in music, dance or theater, playing musical instrument and making art or craft included. Broad participation data only.
- *NEA's Survey of Public Participation in the Arts* — Provides demographic, educational and income information for arts-goers, as well as attendance and participation data for traditional live arts events and alternate forms of participation. Includes data on attendance, media participation, arts performance and creation, arts education, and music and reading preferences.
- *Panel Study of Income Dynamics* — Longitudinal survey that reports demographic data, occupation, income, health and education. Includes

Child Development and Transition to Adulthood supplements with time studies and more detailed information about arts participation and education.

INTERVENING VARIABLES

Arts Creation

Examples of Relevant Studies

- *"Still Kicking: Aging Performing Artists in NYC and LA Metro Areas: Information on Artists IV,"* by Joan Jeffri (2011) — Draws from respondent-driven surveys of performing artists, ages 62 and older, in the New York City and Los Angeles metro areas. The report investigates topics such as access to health insurance, work satisfaction, earnings, and other issues confronting senior performing artists.

- *"Forks in the Road: The Many Paths of Arts Alumni,"* by Strategic National Arts Alumni Project (2011) — Tracks the careers of artists with visual and performing arts degrees, including work in an arts-related field, continued arts production, and use of arts training.

- *"Artists in the Workforce: 1990-2005,"* by NEA Office of Research and Analysis (2008) — Provides employment, income, demographic and geographic information on 11 artistic occupations assembled from U.S. Census Bureau's decennial data and the American Community Survey.

- *"Creative Communities: Artist Data User Guide,"* by Ann Markusen and Greg Schrock (2008) — A guide to tables and maps created by the authors that show tallies of artists for states, metro areas, and public use micro-data areas (PUMAs). The tables and maps draw from the 2000 Decennial Census of Population and include labor force estimates for detailed artist occupations and the share of the area's labor force made up of artists (i.e., location quotients).

- *"Artists' Careers and Their Labor Markets,"* by Neil Alper and Greg Wassall (2006) — Discusses artists' careers and labor market experiences, including available data and methodological issues.

- *"Crossover: How Artists Build Careers across Commercial, Non-profit Work and Community Work,"* by Ann Markusen et al. (2006)

— Explores how each sector is organized in Los Angeles and the Bay Area and how artists move between them. Each sector provides different channels and support for artistic development.

- *"Changing the Beat: A Study of the Worklife of Jazz Musicians,"* by Joan Jeffri (2003) — Examines the demographic make-up, employment and income rates, as well as the work-life of jazz musicians in the U.S.

Examples of Relevant Datasets[5]

- *Bureau of Labor Statistics' Current Population Survey, Occupational Outlook Handbooks, and Current Employment Statistics* — Provides employment, demographic, wage and worker characteristics data by job classification. As of 2002, the Current Population Survey also includes a supplement on volunteer activities.[6]
- *Bureau of Labor Statistics' American Time Use Survey* — Includes employment classifications and time spent on arts and entertainment activities on a given day. Because of the daily measurement, activities are grouped into broader categories.
- *General Social Survey* — Includes demographic, occupational, educational, income, physical and emotional well-being and membership data as part of broad attitudinal survey. 2002 module included more arts-specific data. Membership in art or literary groups, volunteer in arts or culture, arts philanthropy, visit to museum or gallery, visit to internet art sites, performance in music, dance or theater, playing musical instrument and making art or craft included. Broad participation data only.
- *NEA's Survey of Public Participation in the Arts* — Provides demographic, educational and income information for arts-goers, as well as attendance and participation data for traditional live arts events and alternate forms of participation. Includes data on attendance, media participation, arts performance and creation, arts education, and music and reading preferences.
- *U.S. Census Bureau's American Community Survey* — Provides social, economic, housing, and demographic profiles by census tract and block group.
- *U.S. Census Bureau's Decennial Census* — Provides demographic and economic data, including income and occupation, to the census tract level.

Arts Participation

Examples of Relevant Studies

- *"Getting In on the Act: How Arts Groups Are Creating Opportunities for Active Participation,"* by Alan Brown and Jennifer Novak-Leonard (2011) — Examines the redefinition of arts participation and discusses the larger cultural economy. Features case studies exploring individual and community benefits of arts participation.
- *"California's Arts and Cultural Ecology,"* by Ann Markusen, Anne Gadwa, Elisa Barbour, and William Beyers (2011) — Uses a variety of data sets, including the California Cultural Data Project, the American Community Survey, and the Survey of Public Participation in the Arts, to explore the budget sizes, geographic locations, and intrinsic and economic impacts from 11,000 arts and cultural nonprofits in California.
- *"Beyond Attendance: A Multi-modal Understanding of Arts Participation,"* by Jennifer L. Novak-Leonard and Alan Brown (2011) — Study on types of arts participation using data from the Survey of Public Participation in the Arts. Categories include: arts attendance, personal arts creation and performance, and participation through electronic media. Contextual factors include: skill level, form of expression, setting, and degree of creative control. Includes impact of arts education.
- **"Arts Education in America: What the Declines Mean for Arts Participation,"** by Nick Rabkin and E. C. Hedberg (2011) — This report investigates the relationship between arts education and arts participation, based on the Survey of Public Participation in the Arts for 1982, 1992, 2002, and 2008. The report also examines long-term declines in Americans' reported rates of arts learning.
- *"Understanding the Impact of Engagement in Culture and Sport,"* by Mark Newman et al. (2010) — Uses analytical and statistical modeling techniques to begin to understand why people engage or don't engage in cultural and sporting activities, the benefits they obtain from engagement, and the potential value to them and to society as a whole.
- *"Come as You Are: Informal Arts Participation in Urban and Rural Communities,"* by NEA Office of Research and Analysis (2010) — Analyzes data from the Survey of Public Participation in the Arts to assess rural and urban differences in formal and informal arts

participation, particularly between rural and urban areas. Also includes number of nonprofit arts organizations in metro areas.

- *"Engaging Art: What Counts?"* by Steven J. Tepper and Yang Gao *in Engaging in Art: The Next Great Transformation of American's Cultural Life*, eds. Steven Tepper and Bill Ivey (2007) — Proposes a framework that considers multiple forms of social involvement as art participation.
- *"Cultural Indicators for New Zealand,"* by Tohu Ahurea Mö Aotearoa (2006) — Evaluates indicators of the cultural sector to facilitate measurement of its impact with respect to engagement, identity, diversity, social cohesion and economic development.
- *"The Values Study: Rediscovering the Meaning and Value of Arts Participation,"* by Alan Brown (2004) — Discusses five modes of arts participation: inventive, interpretive, curatorial, observational and ambient, as well as the values derived from artistic experiences.
- *"Arts Participation: Steps to Stronger Cultural and Community Life,"* Chris Walker et al. (2003) — Discusses four ways to participate in arts and culture, including the socialization of children as one form of participation.

Examples of Relevant Datasets[7]

- *Bureau of Labor Statistics' American Time Use Survey* — Includes employment classifications and time spent on an average day on education, arts and entertainment. Because of the daily measurement, activities are grouped into broader categories.
- *Bureau of Labor Statistics' Consumer Expenditure Survey* — Provides annual consumer expenditure data, including average household spending.
- *Bureau of Economic Analysis' National Income and Product Accounts* — Provides data on value added by industry, as well as capital, materials, purchased services and employment data. Also provides detail on consumer arts spending.
- *NEA's Survey of Public Participation in the Arts* — Provides demographic, educational and income information for arts-goers, as well as attendance and participation data for traditional live arts events and alternate forms of participation. Includes data on attendance, media participation, arts performance and creation, arts education, and music and reading preferences.

- *General Social Survey* — Includes demographic, occupational, educational, income, physical and emotional well-being and membership data as part of broad attitudinal survey. 2002 module included more arts-specific data. Membership in art or literary groups, volunteer in arts or culture, arts philanthropy, visit to museum or gallery, visit to internet art sites, performance in music, dance or theater, playing musical instrument and making art or craft included. Broad participation data only.
- *Panel Study of Income Dynamics* — Longitudinal survey that reports demographic data, occupation, income, health and education. Includes Child Development and Transition to Adulthood supplements with time studies and more detailed information about arts participation and education.

FIRST-ORDER OUTCOMES

Benefit of Art to Individuals

Examples of Relevant Studies
- *"The Arts and Achievement in At-Risk Youth: Findings from Four Longitudinal Studies,"* by James Catterall et al. (2012) — Study on the benefits of arts education for at-risk children, using longitudinal data from the Departments of Education and Labor. Includes data on civic engagement, graduation rates and labor market outcomes.
- *"Art in Prisons: A Literature Review of the Philosophies and Impacts of Visual Arts Programs for Correctional Populations,"* by Alexandra Djurichkovic (2011) — Literature review examining the impacts of art in prison programs.
- *"The Arts and Human Development: Framing a National Research Agenda for the Arts, Lifelong Learning, and Individual Well-Being,"* by NEA and DHHS (2011) — White paper on the impact of arts on human development at different life stages, including early childhood and older adulthood.
- *"Understanding the Impact of Engagement in Culture and Sport,"* by Mark Newman et al. (2010) — Uses analytical and statistical modeling techniques to begin to understand why people engage or don't engage in cultural and sporting activities, the benefits they

obtain from engagement, and potential value to them and to society as a whole.

- *"Assessing the Intrinsic Impacts of a Live Performance,"* by Alan Brown and Jennifer Novak (2007) — Assesses how audiences are impacted by a live performance. Provides a measurement framework and discusses the audience members' "readiness-to-receive" the art.
- *"Cultural Indicators for New Zealand,"* by Tohu Ahurea Mö Aotearoa (2006) — Evaluates indicators of the cultural sector to facilitate measurement of its impact with respect to engagement, identity, diversity, social cohesion and economic development.
- *"The Values Study: Rediscovering the Meaning and Value of Arts Participation,"* by Alan Brown (2004) — Discusses five modes of arts participation: inventive, interpretive, curatorial, observational and ambient, as well as the values derived from artistic experiences.
- *"Washington, D.C.: Performing Arts Research Coalition Community Report,"* by Mary Kopczynski et al. (2004) — Measures level of participation in and support for the arts in 10 communities across the country.
- *"Gifts of the Muse: Reframing the Debate About the Benefits of the Arts,"* by Kevin McCarthy et al. (2004) — Argues for a broader evaluation of the benefits of the arts beyond the economic to include intrinsic value as well. Charts a continuum of public to private benefits.
- *"How the Arts Impact Communities: An Introduction to the Literature on Arts Impact Studies,"* by Joshua Guetzkow (2002) — Reviews the literature on arts impact studies, including a discussion of theoretical and methodological issues.

Examples of Relevant Datasets[8]

- *General Social Survey* — Includes demographic, occupational, educational, income, physical and emotional well-being and membership data as part of broad attitudinal survey. 2002 module included more arts-specific data. Membership in art or literary groups, volunteer in arts or culture, arts philanthropy, visit to museum or gallery, visit to internet art sites, performance in music, dance or theater, playing musical instrument and making art or craft included. Broad participation data only.

- Panel Study of Income Dynamics — Longitudinal survey that reports demographic data, occupation, income, health and education. Includes Child Development and Transition to Adulthood supplements with time studies and more detailed information about arts participation and education.

Benefit of Art to Society and Communities

Examples of Relevant Studies
- *"How Art Spaces Matter II: The Riverside, Tashiro Kaplan and Insights from Five Artspace Case Studies and Four Cities,"* by Anne Gadwa and Anna Muessig (2011) — Examines case studies of the economic and social impact of arts-based community development.
- *"Creative Partnerships: Intersections between the Arts, Culture and Other Sectors,"* by Annamari Laaksonen (2011) — Explores the ways artists work in diverse settings and the nature of partnerships that exist between the arts and other sectors.
- *"Creative Placemaking,"* by Ann Markusen and Anne Gadwa (2010) — Discusses the role local arts and cultural organizations play in community revitalization and economic development. The report presents case studies ranging from the development of an arts district in Cleveland to the transformation of a vacant Buffalo auto plant into artist studios and housing.
- *"Los Angeles: America's Artist Super City,"* by Ann Markusen (2010) — Evaluates artists' impact on Los Angeles' economy and communities.
- *"From Creative Economy to Creative Society,"* by Mark J. Stern and Susan C. Seifert (2008) — Explores whether the creative economy can ameliorate urban poverty. It suggests that the cultural cluster perspective is the most promising for promoting economic equality and social inclusion.
- *"Cultural Indicators for New Zealand,"* by Tohu Ahurea Mö Aotearoa (2006) — Evaluates indicators of the cultural sector to facilitate measurement of its impact with respect to engagement, identity, diversity, social cohesion and economic development.
- *"Cultural Vitality in Communities: Interpretation and Indicators,"* by Maria Rosario Jackson et al. (2006) — Provides an assessment of

various indicators for the presence of opportunities for cultural participation, cultural participation itself, and support for cultural participation.

- *"The Values Study: Rediscovering the Meaning and Value of Arts Participation,"* by Alan Brown (2004) — Discusses five modes of arts participation: inventive, interpretive, curatorial, observational and ambient, as well as the values derived from artistic experiences.

- *"Capturing Cultural Value,"* by John Holden (2004) — Explores the full range of values expressed through culture, including affective elements, broad public value, public goods. Also discusses methodological issues.

- *"Washington, D.C.: Performing Arts Research Coalition Community Report,"* by Mary Kopczynski et al. (2004) — Measures level of participation in and support for the arts in 10 communities across the country.

- *"Gifts of the Muse: Reframing the Debate About the Benefits of the Arts,"* by Kevin McCarthy et al. (2004) — Argues for a broader evaluation of the benefits of the arts beyond the economic to include intrinsic value as well. Charts a continuum of public to private benefits.

- *"Immigrant Participatory Arts: An Insight into Community-building in Silicon Valley,"* by Pia Moriarty (2004) — Explores informal or "participatory arts," i.e., forms of artistic expression in which everyday people engage in the process of making art.

- *"The Informal Arts: Finding Cohesion, Capacity and Other Cultural Benefits in Unexpected Places,"* by Alaka Wali et al. (2002) — Explores through ethnographic data how informal arts impact the social infrastructure of communities. Includes a definition of building capacity.

- *"How the Arts Impact Communities: An Introduction to the Literature on Arts Impact Studies,"* by Joshua Guetzkow (2002) — Reviews the literature on arts impact studies, including a discussion of theoretical and methodological issues.

Examples of Relevant Datasets[9]

- *NEA's Our Town* — Grant program focused on contributions to creative place-making, with detail from grantees about how the projects promote community livability. Data limited to grantees, but offers detailed information on arts contribution to livability.
- *Social Impact of the Arts Project (SIAP) Cultural Assets Database* — Combines data on the role of arts and culture in urban neighborhoods with information on urban revitalization. Primarily focuses on Philadelphia, although work is also being done on Seattle and Baltimore.
- *U.S. Census Bureau's American Community Survey* — Provides social, economic, housing, and demographic profiles by census tract and block group.
- *USPS Vacancy Survey* — Through an agreement with HUD, provides administrative data on address vacancies at the census tract level.

Direct and Indirect Economic Benefits of Art

Examples of Relevant Studies

- *"How Art Spaces Matter II: The Riverside, Tashiro Kaplan and Insights from Five Artspace Case Studies and Four Cities,"* by Anne Gadwa and Anna Muessig (2011) — Examines case studies of the economic and social impact of arts-based community development.
- *"California's Arts and Cultural Ecology,"* by Ann Markusen, Anne Gadwa, Elisa Barbour, and William Beyers (2011) — Uses a variety of data sets, including the California Cultural Data Project, the American Community Survey, and the Survey of Public Participation in the Arts, to explore the budget sizes, geographic locations, and intrinsic and economic impacts from 11,000 arts and cultural nonprofits in California.
- *"New England's Creative Economy: Nonprofit Sector Impact,"* by New England Foundation for the Arts (2011) — Explores the economic impact of the arts and cultural organizations in New England. Looks at direct, indirect and induced impacts.
- *"Time and Money: Using Federal Data to Measure the Value of Performing Arts Activities,"* by NEA Office of Research and Analysis

(2011) — Examines available datasets useful for monetary and non-monetary value measurements of arts impact.

- *"Arts and the GDP: Value Added by Selected Cultural Industries,"* by NEA Office of Research and Analysis (2011) — Provides data on the economic value added by cultural industries.

- *"Los Angeles: America's Artist Super City,"* by Ann Markusen (2010) — Evaluates artists' impact on Los Angeles' economy and communities.

- *"Arts and Culture in Urban or Regional Planning: A Review and Research Agenda,"* by Ann Markusen and Anne Gadwa in Journal of Planning Education and Research (2010) — Explores arts and culture as an urban or regional development tool, with a focus on the economic impacts of cultural districts and tourist-targeted investments.

- *"Economic Impact of the 2008 American Folk Festival in Bangor, Maine,"* by Bernardita Silva et al. (2009) — Provides an estimate of the economic impact of the 2008 American Folk Festival in Bangor, ME.

- *"Artists in the Workforce: 1990-2005,"* by NEA Office of Research and Analysis (2008) — Provides employment, income, demographic and geographic information on 11 artistic occupations assembled from U.S. Census Bureau's decennial data and the American Community Survey.

- *"From Creative Economy to Creative Society,"* by Mark J. Stern and Susan C. Seifert (2008) — Explores whether the creative economy can ameliorate urban poverty. It suggests that the cultural cluster perspective is the most promising for promoting economic equality and social inclusion.

- *"Cultural Indicators for New Zealand,"* by Tohu Ahurea Mö Aotearoa (2006) — Evaluates indicators of the cultural sector to facilitate measurement of its impact with respect to engagement, identity, diversity, social cohesion and economic development.

- *"Defining the Cultural Economy: Industry and Occupational Approaches,"* by Ann Markusen et al. (2006) — Discusses debates around definitions of creative economies, creative classes, and the regional creative economy.

- *"Economic Impacts of Arts Education,"* by David Throsby (2006) — Discusses the economic and cultural impact of arts education, with a focus on better understanding economic impact.
- *"Gifts of the Muse,"* by Kevin McCarthy et al. (2004) — Argues for a broader evaluation of the benefit of the arts beyond the economic to include intrinsic value as well. Provides a continuum of public to private benefits.
- *"How the Arts Impact Communities: An Introduction to the Literature on Arts Impact Studies,"* by Joshua Guetzkow (2002) — Reviews the literature on arts impact studies, including a discussion of theoretical and methodological issues.
- *"Valuing the Arts: A Contingent Valuation Approach,"* by Eric Thompson et al. (2002) — Uses a contingent valuation method to assess how much individuals monetarily value the arts.

Examples of Relevant Datasets[10]

- *Bureau of Economic Analysis' National Income and Product Accounts* — Provides data on value added by industry, as well as capital, materials, purchased services and employment data. Also provides detail on consumer arts spending.
- *Bureau of Labor Statistics' Current Population Survey, Occupational Outlook Handbooks, and Current Employment Statistics* — Provides employment, demographic, wage and worker characteristics data by job classification. As of 2002, the Current Population Survey also includes a supplement on volunteer activities.[11]
- *Bureau of Labor Statistics' Consumer Expenditure Survey* — Provides annual consumer expenditure data, including average household spending.
- *IRS Tax Statistics* — Data aggregated to zip-code level, with entity numbers, receipts and net income at the Arts, Entertainment and Recreation level. Form 990 data is available for tax-exempt organizations.
- *National Center for Charitable Statistics' (NCCS) Unified Database of Arts Organizations (UDAO)* — Provides a master list of commercial, nonprofit, and governmental organizations with arts programs.
- *NEA's Our Town* — Grant program focused on contributions to creative place-making, with detail from grantees about how the

projects promote community livability. Data limited to grantees, but offers detailed information on arts contribution to livability.

- *U.S. Census Bureau's American Community Survey* — Provides social, economic, housing, and demographic profiles by census tract and block group.
- *U.S. Census Bureau's County Business Patterns* — Provides sub-national economic data by industry, including number of employees, type of organization and payroll.
- *U.S. Census Bureau's Economic Census* — Provides economic data on performing arts, museum and historical sites, including number of establishments, receipt and employment data.
- *U.S. Census Bureau's Nonemployer Statistics* — Offers sub-national economic data by industry, including number of businesses and total receipts, for businesses that have no paid employees.

SECOND-ORDER OUTCOME VARIABLES

Societal Capacities to Innovate and Express Ideas

Examples of Relevant Studies
- *"It Takes a Village: A Test of the Creative Class, Social Capital, and Human Capital Theories,"* by Michele Hoyman and Christopher Faricy (2009) — Explores the concept of creative class and does not find evidence that creative class is related to growth, whereas human capital predicts economic growth.
- *"The Creative Class: A Key to Rural Growth,"* by David McGranahan and Timothy Wojan (2007) — Discusses the creative class in the context of rural development.
- *"Defining the Cultural Economy: Industry and Occupational Approaches,"* by Ann Markusen et al. (2006) — Discusses debates around definitions of creative economies, creative classes and the regional creative economy.
- *"Cities and the Creative Class,"* by Richard Florida (2003) — Discusses the concept of creative class as a driver of regional growth.
- *"The Informal Arts: Finding Cohesion, Capacity and Other Cultural Benefits in Unexpected Places,"* by Alaka Wali et al. (2002) — Explores, through ethnographic data, how informal arts can affect the

social infrastructure of communities. Includes a definition of building capacity.

Examples of Relevant Datasets[12]

- *Bureau of Labor Statistics' Current Population Survey, Occupational Outlook Handbooks, and Current Employment Statistics* — Provides employment, demographic, wage and worker characteristics data by job classification. As of 2002, the Current Population Survey also includes a supplement on volunteer activities.[13]
- *U.S. Census Bureau's American Community Survey* — Provides social, economic, housing, and demographic profiles by census tract and block group.

APPENDIX B

Process

The How Art Works chapter consisted of two phases. In Phase I we conducted a series of interviews with experts inside and outside the world of art. In Phase II we engaged in several convenings and web meetings to pressure test our system map and brainstorm measurement approaches. (See illustration below for a graphical representation of the process.)

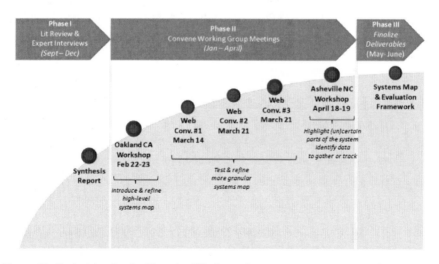

Figure 11. Project arc for the How Art Works project.

Participants

The following individuals participated as interviewees and workshop and webinar participants:

Alaka Wali, Director, Center for Cultural Understanding and Change, The Field Museum
Alan Brown, Consultant, WolfBrown
Alice io Oglesby, Board Member, Asheville Chamber of Commerce
Amy Kitchener , Living Cultures Grants Program Manager, Alliance for Californian Traditional Arts
Andrew Taylor, Director, Bolz Center for Arts Administration, University of Wisconsin
Andrew Zolli, Futurist, Founder, Z+ partners
Angel Ciangi, Consumer Researcher, The Intelligence Group
Arlene Goldbard, Consultant
Becky Anderson, Founder and Former Director, Hand Made in America
Chall Gray, Owner, The Magnetic Field Restaurant and Black Box Theater
Charlie Flynn-McIver, Director, North Carolina Stage Co.
C.J. Hirschfield, Executive Director, Children's Fairyland
Craig McAnsh, President and Creative Director, Native Marketing
Dana Powell Russell, Independent Evaluation Consultant
Daniel Glaser, Head of Special Projects, Public Engagement, Wellcome Trust
David Sibbet, Graphic Recorder, Founder and President, The Grove Consultants International
David Starkey, Founder, Artistic and General Director, Asheville Lyric Opera
Deborah Sherman, Contributor, Oak Town Art
Diane Driessen, Art Teacher, Friends School Mullica Hill
Don Derosby, Senior Consultant, Global Business Network
Douglas Nickel, Curator and Professor, Brown University
Elizabeth Streb, Dancer and Managing Director, S.L.A.M. (Streb Laboratories for Action Mechanics)
Erika Gregory, Founder, President, Collective Invention
Gong Szeto, Designer Co-Founder and CEO, Doxa2, Inc
Hilary Austen, Adjunct Professor, Rotman School of Management
Holly Block, Director and Former Curator, Bronx Museum
Isaac Prilleltensky, Dean of the School of Education, University of Miami
Jaime Cortez, Writer, Editor, Painter, Activist
Jane Prophet, Mixed Media Artist

Jeffrey Coates, National Program Associate, The Knight Foundation

Jeff Marley, Fine and Heritage Arts Coordinator, Southwestern Community College

John Ellis, Managing Director, Diana Wortham Theater

John Holden, Associate, Former Head of Culture, DEMOS

John Maeda, Graphic Designer and Computer Scientist, President, Rhode Island School of Design

Joseph Chamie, Former Researcher, Center for Migration Studies

Karen Tessier, Board Member, Pack Square Park Conservancy

Keri Putnam, Executive Director, Sundance Institute

Kitty Love, Executive Director, Asheville Area Arts Council

Kristin Marting, Co-Founder and Artistic Director, HERE Arts Center

Laura Boosinger, Folk Singer, Traditional Folk Artist, Independent

Laurie Schell, Founding Principal, Laurie Schell Associates

Libby Schaaf, Councilmember, Oakland City Council

Linda Walton, Vice President of Programming, Jazzmobile

Lisa Kay Solomon, Adjunct Professor, Innovation Studio, California College of the Arts and Stanford

Business School

Luis Rodriguez, Slam Artist and Founder, Tia Chucha's Centro Cultural

Marc Bamuthi Joseph , Artistic Director, Youth Speaks

Maria Rosario Jackson, Senior Research Associate, Metropolitan Housing and Communities Policy

Center, Urban Institute

Marian Godfrey, Senior Director, Cultural Initiatives, Pew Charitable Trusts

Marjorie McGuirk, Meteorologist, National Climatic Data Center

Michael Edson, Director of Web and New Media Strategy, Smithsonian Institute

Michelle Moog-Koussa, Executive Director, Bob Moog Foundation

Nicole Neditch, Independent Curator, Graphic Designer, and Arts Administrator

Nolan Gasser, Chief Music Architect, Pandora

Randy Shull, Co-founder, Creative Director, and Artist, Pink Dog Creative

Raquel Paiewonsky, Modern Artist

Regie Gibson, Poet, Songwriter, Author, Workshop Facilitator, and Educator

Rene De Guzman, Senior Curator, Oakland Museum

Robert Hauser, Executive Director, National Academies

Rosalba Rolon, Founder and Artistic Director, Pregones Theater

Sally Jo Fifer, President and CEO, ITVS

Sandra Vivanco, Architect, A+D and California College of the Arts

Scott Spann, Founder, Innate Strategies

Sean Pace, Co-Founder and Visual Artist, Flood Gallery and Fine Arts Center

Sharon West, Board Member, YMI Cultural Center

Thomas Skeffington, Potter and Ceramic Artist, and Professor of Art, Rowan University

Steven Huss, Cultural Arts Manager , City of Oakland Cultural Arts and Marketing Division

Steven Weber, Professor, UC Berkeley School of Information

Steven Young, Executive Director, The Crucible

Summer Brenner, Community-Based Fiction Writer

Sydney Cooper, Mixed Media Artist, Unaffiliated

Theaster Gates, Visual Artist and Cultural Planner, Independent

Tim Brown, CEO and President, IDEO

Tom Reis, Retired, Venture Philanthropy Director, W.K. Kellogg Foundation (retired)

Victor Palomino, Community-based artist, Mixed Media Artist

End Notes

[1] Many data sets can be accessed through The Cultural Policy and the National Arts Data Archive (CPANDA), which has extracts of larger data sets that relate directly to the arts.

[2] Due to U.S. Census reclassification, occupational data beginning in January 2011 is not strictly comparable to data from earlier years. See Bureau of Labor Statistics, "Occupational and Industry Classification Systems Used in the Current Population Survey." For more on arts data from the Occupational Outlook Handbooks, see National Endowment for the Arts. 2011. "Artist Employment Projections through 2018." Research Note #103. June 27.

[3] This reference is not available in the original document.

[4] Many data sets can be accessed through The Cultural Policy and the National Arts Data Archive (CPANDA), which has extracts of larger data sets that relate directly to the arts.

[5] Many data sets can be accessed through The Cultural Policy and the National Arts Data Archive (CPANDA), which has extracts of larger data sets that relate directly to the arts.

[6] Due to U.S. Census reclassification, occupational data beginning in January 2011 is not strictly comparable to data from earlier years. See Bureau of Labor Statistics, "Occupational and Industry Classification Systems Used in the Current Population Survey." For more on arts data from the Occupational Outlook Handbooks, see National Endowment for the Arts. 2011. "Artist Employment Projections through 2018." Research Note #103. June 27.

[7] Many data sets can be accessed through The Cultural Policy and the National Arts Data Archive (CPANDA), which has extracts of larger data sets that relate directly to the arts.

[8] Many data sets can be accessed through The Cultural Policy and the National Arts Data Archive (CPANDA), which has extracts of larger data sets that relate directly to the arts.

[9] Many data sets can be accessed through The Cultural Policy and the National Arts Data Archive (CPANDA), which has extracts of larger data sets that relate directly to the arts.

[10] Many data sets can be accessed through The Cultural Policy and the National Arts Data Archive (CPANDA), which has extracts of larger data sets that relate directly to the arts.

[11] Due to U.S. Census reclassification, occupational data beginning in January 2011 is not strictly comparable to data from earlier years. See Bureau of Labor Statistics, "Occupational and Industry Classification Systems Used in the Current Population Survey." For more on arts data from the Occupational Outlook Handbooks, see National Endowment for the Arts. 2011. "Artist Employment Projections through 2018." Research Note #103. June 27.

[12] Many data sets can be accessed through The Cultural Policy and the National Arts Data Archive (CPANDA), which has extracts of larger data sets that relate directly to the arts.

[13] Due to U.S. Census reclassification, occupational data beginning in January 2011 is not strictly comparable to data from earlier years. See Bureau of Labor Statistics, "Occupational and Industry Classification Systems Used in the Current Population Survey." For more on arts data from the Occupational Outlook Handbooks, see National Endowment for the Arts. 2011. "Artist Employment Projections through 2018." Research Note #103. June 27.

In: Measuring the Arts
Editors: K. O'Connell and D. Myrick

ISBN: 978-1-62618-269-1
© 2013 Nova Science Publishers, Inc.

Chapter 3

THE ARTS AND HUMAN DEVELOPMENT: FRAMING A NATIONAL RESEARCH AGENDA FOR THE ARTS, LIFELONG LEARNING AND INDIVIDUAL WELL-BEING[*]

Gay Hanna, Michael Patterson, Judy Rollins and Andrea Sherman

EXECUTIVE SUMMARY

Overview

Human development describes a complex web of factors affecting the health and well-being of individuals across the lifespan. Together, these factors yield cognitive and behavioral outcomes that can shape the social and economic circumstances of individuals, their levels of creativity and productivity, and overall quality of life.

Increasingly in the 21st century, U.S. policy leaders in health and education have recognized a need for strategies and interventions to address "the whole person." They have urged a more integrated approach to policy development—one that can reach Americans at various stages of their lives, across generations, and in multiple learning contexts.

---

[*] This white paper was released by the National Endowment for the Arts, November 2011.

The arts are ideally suited to promote this integrated approach. In study after study, arts participation and arts education have been associated with improved cognitive, social, and behavioral outcomes in individuals *across the lifespan*: in early childhood, in adolescence and young adulthood, and in later years. The studies include:

- Neuroscience research showing strong connections between arts learning and improved cognitive development;
- Small comparison group studies revealing the arts' contributions to school-readiness in early childhood;
- Longitudinal data analyses demonstrating positive academic and social outcomes for at-risk teenagers who receive arts education; and
- Several studies reporting improvements in cognitive function and self-reported quality of life for older adults who engage in the arts and creative activities, compared to those who do not.

This emerging body of evidence appears to support a need for greater integration of arts activities into health and educational programs for children, youth, and older adults. Yet further research is necessary so that policy-makers and practitioners can understand the pathways and processes by which the arts affect human development, thereby enhancing the efficacy of arts-based practices in optimizing health and educational outcomes for Americans of all ages.

NEA-HHS Collaboration

On March 14, 2011, the National Endowment for the Arts (NEA) in partnership with the U.S. Department of Health and Human Services (HHS) hosted a convening in Washington, DC to showcase some of the nation's most compelling studies and evidence-based programs that have identified cognitive, social, and behavioral outcomes from arts interventions.

HHS Secretary Kathleen Sebelius and NEA Chairman Rocco Landesman gave keynote speeches, followed by senior officials representing the HHS Administration for Children and Families (ACF) and Administration on Aging (AoA). Representatives from the National Institutes of Health (NIH) and the Health Resources and Services Administration (HRSA) also participated. The NEA Office of Research and Analysis organized the event.

Secretary Sebelius declared a mutual goal for the convening agencies: "We hope this meeting leads to deeper collaboration in research and in

The Arts and Human Development 83

identifying new ways to engage the arts to improve people's lives." Similarly, Chairman Landesman asked: "How do the arts help build us as a people and as individuals?" The NEA and HHS, he said, "share a fundamental mission—how to improve the quality of life."

The resulting white paper proposes a framework for long-term collaboration among the NEA, HHS, and other federal agencies to build capacity for future research and evidence-sharing about the arts' role in human development. A worthy aim of that collaboration is to foster data-driven models for including the arts in policies and programs that seek to improve the well-being of Americans at different stages of their lives.

Key Research Findings

Studies reported at the convening and elsewhere have measured cognitive, social, and behavioral development among arts participants and arts learners. The research applies to three pivotal sections of the lifespan:

Early Childhood
- Three- to five-year-olds from low socioeconomic status (SES) families demonstrated significant gains in nonverbal IQ, numeracy, and spatial cognition after they had received music training and attention training in a small-class setting—compared to a regular Head Start control group (Neville, et al. 2008).
- Students from low-income backgrounds who attended an "arts enrichment" preschool improved in school-readiness skills, more so after two years than after one year of program attendance. Children from diverse racial and ethnic backgrounds benefited equally. In a related study by the same research team, students attending the arts enrichment preschool showed higher levels of language development (measured by "receptive vocabulary") than did students who attended a comparison preschool (Brown, Benedett, and Armistead 2010).
- Children attending a preschool that used an arts integration model made greater developmental strides in multiple domains, including initiative, social relations, creative representation, music and move-ment, language, literacy, and logic and mathematics, compared to children in a regular Head Start program (Social Dynamics, LLC 2005).

Youth and Adolescence

- Arts-engaged low-income students were more likely than their non-arts-engaged peers to attend and do well in college, obtain employment, volunteer in their communities, and participate in the political process by voting. Study findings suggest that arts-engaged low-income students performed similarly to average higher-income students (Catterall 2009).
- Student behavior, measured by numbers of suspensions and discipline referrals, improved in schools involved in an arts integration initiative, as did student attendance. Student academic achievement also improved: seventh-grade students in treatment schools significantly outperformed control-group students on state standardized tests in reading and math (Pittsburgh Public Schools ca. 2008).
- Students involved in after-school activities at arts organizations demonstrated greater use of complex language than did their peers. Students who were involved in arts education for at least nine hours a week were four times more likely than their peers nationally to have won school-wide recognition for their academic achievement and three times more likely to have won an award for school attendance (Heath 1999).

Older Adults

- Older adults participating in a chorale program reported higher overall physical health, fewer doctor visits, less medication use, fewer instances of falls, and fewer health problems when compared to a control group. The chorale group also displayed evidence of higher morale and less loneliness than did the control group (Cohen, et al. 2006).
- Older adults participating in a structured theatrical intervention over four weeks significantly improved, compared to two control groups (a singing group and a no-treatment control group) in four cognitive measures: immediate word recall, problem-solving, verbal fluency, and delayed recall (Noice and Noice 2009).
- Older adults with Alzheimer's disease and those with related dementias who participated in a creative storytelling intervention became more engaged and more alert than those in a control group. There were more frequent staff-resident interactions, peer social interactions, and social engagement in facilities using the creative

storytelling intervention than in control-group facilities (Fritsch, et al. 2009).

Challenges and Opportunities

Although these findings are promising, convening participants agreed that a collective leap forward is necessary to a) replicate, extend, and bring such studies to scale and b) share the results with researchers, practitioners, and the general public. In particular, the following challenges remain:

- *A lack of coordination* among federal agency departments and investigators and practitioners from various disciplines (e.g., arts education, child development, medicine, nursing, educational psychology, cognitive neuroscience, the behavioral and social sciences) in pursuing a vigorous research agenda to understand the role of arts and arts education in human development.
- *The small size of study populations* participating in research on the arts and human development currently limits generalizability of the results. So far, the majority of reported studies rely on correlational data, rather than results from well-controlled trials. Another limiting factor is the dearth of longitudinal studies.
- *Low visibility of research findings*, program evaluation data, and evidence-based models integrating the arts in health and educational programs provided at various segments of the lifespan.

These needs have acquired greater currency in light of recent demographic trends and domestic policy priorities. With a rising cohort of highly active baby-boomers facing retirement, opportunities for creative engagement and lifelong learning in the arts are likely to prove critical for improved health and well-being. Educators and communities, confronted with large percentages of Americans failing to finish high school, are seeking innovative and effective strategies to engage students and boost their achievement levels. In this climate, a stronger role for arts education should be investigated.

Finally, the high-order critical thinking and creativity skills that have been linked to arts training are deemed increasingly vital to today's workforce, the U.S. economy, and our nation's overall competitiveness. At the convening, Mary Wright, a program director with the Conference Board, asserted: "Creativity and innovation are going to increase in importance."

Wright based her conclusion on recent industry surveys of employers' hiring needs. The results are clear: U.S. companies stand to gain from the knowledge and skills that an arts education can provide. High demand among employers for creativity, innovation, and critical thinking will translate into positive social and economic outcomes for workers who possess those skills, thus contributing more broadly to their human development.

Recommendations

The moment is ripe for federal leadership in the design, conduct, and dissemination of rigorous research and evidence-based practices documenting the arts' contributions to human development—from early childhood, adolescence, and young adulthood to middle-aged and older adults.

To support this leadership role, the following actions are recommended:

1. Establish a federal interagency task force to promote the regular sharing of research and information about the arts and human development.

The task force would include high-level officials from the National Endowment for the Arts, the Department of Education, and HHS agencies such as the Administration for Children and Families, the Administration on Aging, and the National Institutes of Health. The group would convene two to three times a year to review progress on the following tasks:

- *Host a series of webinars* highlighting examples of compelling research and evidence-based practices that have integrated the arts in human development. The webinars will be available to the public, but aimed especially at researchers and providers of the arts, health, and education for various segments of the lifespan.
- *Coordinate the distribution of information* about funding opportunities for researchers and providers of the arts, health, and education across the lifespan.
- *Conduct or commission an inventory and gap analysis* of federally sponsored research on the arts and human development so that future research opportunities can be developed by and across agencies, departments, and the private sector.
- *Develop an online clearinghouse* of research and evidence-based practices that examine or utilize the arts in health and educational programs across the lifespan.

The Arts and Human Development

2. Convene a series of technical workshops to help develop research proposals that represent robust and innovative study design methods to investigate the relationship between the arts and human development. If the most competitive research proposals are to reach the appropriate funders, both public and private, then capacity-building through peer learning must occur. A series of workshops would help to improve the overall rigor of such studies, by recruiting outstanding scientists to tackle vexing and complex problems in pursuing this topic. Because of formidable difficulties involved in mounting large-scale, longitudinal studies of the arts at work in human development—and because of the complexity of study design factors related to different age populations—it is important to bring together research methodologists and content experts in neuroscience, health, education, and the arts to advance discussion of key topics, including:

- *What are appropriate outcomes* (including quality-of-life indicators) for studies comparing arts interventions with control groups in the provision of health and/or educational services?
- *How might successful randomization be achieved* and comparison research designs developed for exploring the arts' potential impact, particularly on children and older adults?
- *How can diversity in the study populations be promoted* to ensure that findings about the arts and human development will apply toward and thus potentially benefit all groups (i.e., individuals from all ages and racial/ethnic backgrounds, including those with disabilities)?
- *How can artists and arts educators contribute fully* to the planning and conduct of research? What protocols and criteria should guide the administration of arts content and delivery?

3. Bring the arts to national and international conversations about integrating the concept of well-being into policy development. Even while new evidence is being gathered, the federal partnership should leverage growing national and international interest in using measures of subjective well-being as complementary and valuable tools to guide policy decisions. This discussion is highly consistent with the HHS strategic goal—"Advance the health, safety, and well-being of the American people." At the same time, greater analysis of the arts in direct relationship to well-being will provide the NEA with an opportunity to realize one of its own strategic goals for the American people—"Promote public knowledge and understanding about the contributions of the arts." This recommendation also aligns with two National

Institute on Aging-sponsored efforts to advance the measurement of subjective well-being for application to research on aging and health. Those efforts include:

- Development of a National Research Council panel on "measuring subjective well-being in a policy-relevant framework." This initiative, co-sponsored by the UK Economic and Social Research Council, was singled out by the White House in a May 25, 2011, joint fact sheet as having "the potential to generate new insights that will directly inform social and economic policies."
- A series of National Academies workshops that will conclude in September 2012 with recommendations on the "evaluation of measures of subjective wellbeing and development of OECD (Organization for Economic Co-operation and Development) guidance for national statistical agencies on the measurement of well-being." The workshops should be monitored for their potential applicability to future federal data collection about the arts' role in human development.

Ultimately, it may surprise no one to discover that arts and arts education have strong positive effects on wellness and quality of life. Throughout human history, in virtually all cultures, the arts have been viewed as a hallmark of civilization—so why not of health and human development? Yet one thing is certain: without vigorous and extensive research and evidence-sharing among government agencies, scientists, practitioners, and the general public, our nation will continue to lack effective, replicable models for using the arts to improve quality-of-life outcomes. The resulting deficiency represents a substantial loss for arts, health, and education providers serving Americans at all stages of life. The NEA-HHS partnership, through this white paper, endorses the timeliness and potential cost-effectiveness of the proposed collaborations and research endeavors.

INTRODUCTION

Increasingly in the 21st century, U.S. policy leaders in health and education have recognized a need for strategies and interventions to address the development of the "whole person." They have urged a more integrated approach to policy development—one that can reach Americans at various stages of their lives, across generations, and in multiple learning contexts. The recent surge of interest in measurements of happiness and subjective well-being also reflects a growing desire to assess multiple dimensions of human development.[1] Participation in the arts and arts learning has long been believed to support the development of human potential. Harvard psychologist Howard Gardner, in his 1983 book, *Frames of Mind,* proposed that we as individuals have multiple intelligences. These ways of knowing are influenced by a preferred sensory modality: one person may learn and develop better through listening or auditory experiences, whereas another may need to learn kinesthetically or visually or use multimodal learning. Involvement in the arts and arts learning increases an individual's exposure to multiple ways of experiencing the world, and, in so doing, increases the potential for human development. Over the past two decades, landmark studies have associated arts participation and arts education with cognitive, social, and behavioral advantages in individuals across the lifespan: in early childhood, in adolescence and young adulthood, and in later years. For example, some studies have linked the arts to school-readiness, academic achievement, and lower risks of juvenile delinquency. Other studies, concerning the latter part of life, have shown that arts engagement and arts learning have the potential to reduce the need for medication, reduce falls by improving gait and balance, and improve brain fitness. A sample of these studies are summarized in the chapters that follow. Until quite recently, it was not clearly understood how the arts contribute to these outcomes. Research in the field of cognitive neuroscience has begun to make significant strides in this area. In his keynote address at the March 14, 2011, NEA-HHS event, Dr. Michael Gazzaniga, a nationally renowned cognitive neuroscientist, recounted the significant Dana Foundation-supported *Learning, Arts, and the Brain* research initiative. The effort united cognitive neuroscientists from seven universities across North America "to grapple with the question of why arts training has been associated with higher academic performance."[2] One critical mechanism that might explain enhanced cognition, he said, is exercise of the brain's attentional network:

> We know that the brain has a system of neuropathways dedicated for attention.... We know that training these attention networks improves general measures of intelligence. We can be fairly sure that focusing our attention on learning and performing an art, if we practice frequently and are truly engaged, activates these same attentional networks. We, therefore, would expect focused training in the arts to improve cognition generally.[3]

The findings from *Learning, Arts, and the Brain* illustrate Gazzaniga's expression of the relationship between arts learning and improved cognitive outcomes. In assessing this relationship with respect to music and mathematical ability, one study found that intensive music training for children and adolescents is associated with an improved ability to represent abstract geometry.[4] These findings expand on earlier studies showing that music training enhanced preschool children's spatial-temporal reasoning.[5] In other research generated by the Dana Foundation initiative, involvement in arts training was associated with greater ability to focus attention.[6]

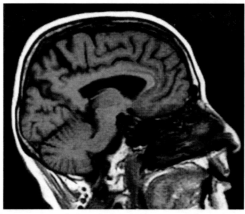

Cognitive neuroscience research has informed our understanding of the role of arts education in cultivating creativity. In a study published in 2008, Ansari and Berkowitz used functional magnetic resonance imaging (fMRI) to examine musical improvisation in university-level music majors.[7] Participants played melodies—both rehearsed and improvised—on a fiber-optic keyboard. The study found that during improvisation, the highly trained music majors used their brains in a way the non-musicians could not: they deactivated their right-temporoparietal junction. Music majors were able to block all distractions, allowing them to concentrate to a greater degree and create music spontaneously. The study findings demonstrate a positive relationship between music training and improvisational ability, suggesting, as experimental psychologist James Kaufman has asserted, that "creativity can be taught".[8]

Cultivating Creativity.

In study after study presented during the NEA-HHS convening and elsewhere, arts participation and arts education have been linked with cognitive, social, and behavioral outcomes in individuals across the lifespan. This growing body of evidence, presented in the sections that follow, applies

The Arts and Human Development 91

to three pivotal segments: early childhood, youth and adolescents, and older adults. Still, as detailed in this chapter, there are considerable gaps in our knowledge about the particular pathways and processes by which the arts affect human development. Are such benefits unique to the arts, for example, or are they more strongly associated with other factors or interventions? Only through further research will policymakers and practitioners acquire the ability to enhance the efficacy of arts-based practices in optimizing health and educational outcomes for Americans of all ages.

End Notes

[1] See, for instance, the announcement of the involvement of the United Kingdom's Economic and Social Research Council in partnership with the National Institute on Aging at the National Institutes of Health in the development of a U.S. National Research Council Panel on measuring subjective well-being in a policy-relevant framework: http://www.whitehouse. gov/the-press-office/2011/05/25/joint-factsheet-us-uk-higher-education

[2] Michael Gazzaniga, "Arts and Cognition: Finding Hints in Relationships," in *Learning, Arts, and the Brain,* eds. Carolyn Asbury and Barbara Rich, v.

[3] Michael S. Gazzaniga, "Music, Science and the Art of Living." Panel discussion at "The Arts and Human Development: Learning across the Lifespan," a convening by the National Endowment for the Arts in partnership with the U.S. Department of Health and Human Services, Washington, DC, March 2011.

[4] Elizabeth Spelke, "Effects of Music Instruction on Developing Cognitive Systems at the Foundations of Mathematics and Science," in *Learning, Arts, and the Brain,* eds. Carolyn Asbury and Barbara Rich, 17–49.

[5] Frances H. Rauscher, G.L. Shaw, L.J. Levine, E.L. Wright, W.R. Dennis, and R.L. Newcomb, "Music Training Causes Long-Term Enhancement of Preschool Children's Spatial-Temporal Reasoning," *Neurological Research,* 19 (1997): 2–8.

[6] Helen Neville, et al., "Effects of Music Training on Brain and Cognitive Development in Under-Privileged 3- to 5-Year-Old Children: Preliminary Results," in *Learning, Arts, and the Brain,* eds. Carolyn Asbury and Barbara Rich, 105–116.

[7] Aaron L. Berkowitz and Daniel Ansari, "Generation of novel motor sequences: The neural correlates of musical improvisation," *NeuroImage* 41(2) (2008): 535–543.

[8] Po Bronson and Ashley Merryman, "The Creativity Crisis," *Newsweek,* July 10, 2010, accessed August 8, 2011, http://www.thedailybeast.com/ newsweek/2010/07/10/the-creativity-crisis.html.

THE ARTS IN EARLY CHILDHOOD

The growth of the human brain during early childhood is remarkable. By age three, a child's brain is 90 percent of its adult size.[1]

In these early years, young children reach developmental milestones that include emotional regulation and attachment, language development, and motor skills. When a young child experiences environmental stressors and other negative risk factors, all of the milestones can be significantly delayed and may seriously compromise the child's growth and development.

Of Erik Erikson's three major stages of child development (early childhood, middle childhood, and adolescence), early childhood is increasingly recognized as providing the foundation for lifelong health, learning, and well-being.[2]

Usually defined as birth to year eight, early childhood is not only a time of tremendous physical, cognitive, and social-emotional development—it also strongly influences school-readiness and later success in life.[3]

Traditionally, the arts have been an important part of early-childhood programs. Friedrich Froebel, who developed the concept of kindergarten, believed that young children should be involved both in making their own art and enjoying the art of others. To Froebel, art activities were important not because they allowed teachers to recognize children with unusual abilities, but because they encouraged each child's "full, all-round development."[4]

Today, although most scholars and practitioners agree that arts education enhances artistic skills and development of the "whole child,"[5] others propose that it contributes to the development of specific skills and behaviors.[6] Mounting evidence suggests that the arts prime or stimulate specific cognitive skills.[7]

Music instruction, for example, seems to develop specific spatial-temporal skills.[8] Other research indicates that the arts may advance children's school-readiness.[9]

Evidence also suggests that the arts can improve learning for children most at risk for poor educational outcomes.

At the same time, research about the benefits of the arts in other important areas, such as helping children cope with normative stressors and those associated with illness, injury, disability, and healthcare experiences, is relatively scarce.

Despite these promising avenues for research, we still need to understand more about the basic pathways through which the arts may effect changes in cognitive development and school-readiness.

Are the arts themselves—for example, music, visual arts, and drama—integral to those benefits, or do other factors such as small classroom size and intense adult attention play a greater role in achieving such outcomes?

Evidence-Based Claims

The following studies exemplify the state of current evidence supporting the benefits of art and arts education for young children.

1. Rauscher, et al. (1997): The authors described the results of a study involving 78 children who were enrolled in preschool classes. The children were assigned to one of four groups: private piano keyboard lessons and casual singing, casual daily singing, private computer lessons, and no lessons. Keyboard and computer lessons were matched in frequency and duration. The children received pre- and post-tests for spatial-temporal reasoning and spatial recognition skills.

The Settlement Music School's Kaleidoscope Preschool Arts Enrichment Program, which serves as a Philadelphia Head Start site, operates from 8:45 a.m. to 3:00 p.m. each day, five days a week, 40 weeks a year. The daily schedule includes early-learning classes found in a typical Head Start program as well as arts classes in music, dance, or creative movement, and visual arts classes taught by fully credentialed artist teachers in separate artist studios. The classes are designed to foster development of artistic skills and skills in core cognitive domains that represent traditional early-learning content areas of math, science, language, literacy, and social and cultural awareness. Instruction is centered on early-learning themes. For example, if the theme is shapes, then children might label shapes in their early-learning class, choose musical instruments of different shapes, draw shapes in a visual arts class, or make shapes with their bodies through dance or creative movement.

Settlement Music School.

Results of the study showed that children who participated in the keyboard classes improved significantly on spatial-temporal reasoning while children in the other three groups did not. The magnitude of the spatial-temporal improvement from keyboard training was greater than one standard deviation of the standardized test. However, no significant score improvement was found in spatial recognition for any of the groups.

2. Social Dynamics, LLC (2005): This evaluation study measured the effectiveness and quality of Fairfax Pages, a teacher-residency program administered by Vienna, Virginia-based Wolf Trap Institute for Early Learning through the Arts. The impact evaluation portion of this study was designed to assess whether the program resulted in teacher adoption of Wolf Trap's approach to integration of performing arts-based learning experiences with existing preschool curricula. The impact evaluation also included a quasi-experimental comparison group study, which measured the developmental progress of children between baseline (September 2004) and follow-up (June 2005) observations.

The observational instrument—the Preschool Child Observation Record—measured young children's knowledge and abilities in six domains: Initiative, Social Relations, Creative Representation, Music and Movement, Language and Literacy, and Logic and Mathematics. Statistically significant differences between the treatment and comparison-group children's scores in all six domains favored the treatment group. There were also statistically significant differences favoring the treatment group in the other five domains of knowledge and ability.

3. Neville, et al. (2008): For an article that appeared in *Learning, Arts, and the Brain: The Dana Consortium Report of Arts and Cognition*, Helen Neville and her colleagues examined the effects of music training on brain and cognitive development in 88 children enrolled in Head Start preschools. The children were three to five years old and from low socioeconomic status (SES) backgrounds. They were assigned to either a small group that focused on music activities, such as listening to, moving to, and making music, as well as singing; or to one of three control groups. The first two control groups were either a large or small class where students received regular Head Start instruction. The third control group was a small class in which children received training in focusing attention and becoming more aware of details.

Children in each of the four groups were tested prior to and after participation in the eight-week classes on a wide variety of measures, including language fundamentals, vocabulary, letter identification, IQ, spatial cognition, and developmental numeracy. Results showed that children who received music training and those with attention training showed strong and significant improvements in non-verbal IQ, numeracy, and spatial cognition. Children enrolled in the small Head Start class also displayed large improvements on the same measures. These improvements were not seen in children who received regular Head Start instruction in the large-class control group. The authors concluded that increased time in a small group with intense adult attention, including attention focused through music training, may produce improvements in young children's cognitive abilities.

4. Brown, Benedett, and Armistead (2010): In *Early Childhood Research Quarterly*, Eleanor Brown and her colleagues reported results from two studies. Study 1 used a quasi-experimental design to compare end-of-attendance achievement for children with one year versus two years of program attendance in an arts enrichment program. Students practiced school-readiness skills through early learning, music, creative movement, and visual arts classes. Study 2 compared the arts enrichment program to another high-quality preschool program on an outcome measure of "receptive vocabulary," which is predictive of school success and general intelligence.

Results from Study 1 found that students who attended the preschool for two years demonstrated higher achievement than those who attended for one year, suggesting that the program dosage matters. Among all race/ethnicity and developmental-level groups, students improved in school-readiness skills. Study 2 found that students attending the arts program had higher receptive vocabulary scores than did children at the comparison school.

Looking to the Future

Research suggests that the arts can boost learning in young children, improve their cognitive skills, and help young children facing the greatest risks of poor educational outcomes. Still, rigorous research about the benefits of the arts in other important areas is critically needed.

- *Gap:* Research should investigate the role of the arts in helping young children to cope with normative stressors and those that result from illness, injury, disability, and healthcare experiences.

The current evidence suggests that young children who have the opportunity to learn and participate in the arts develop critical thinking and metacognitive skills and can learn to think creatively. Furthermore, there is a fundamental assumption that this type of arts engagement promotes changes in the brain, which, in turn, support creative thinking and creative expression.

- *Gap:* Research and evaluation is needed to determine how engagement in arts and arts training shapes the neurological structure and function of young minds.
- *Gap:* Further research into creative processes and activities is needed to better understand the emerging neurological substrates of creative thinking. What supports highly creative brain functioning? How can environmental influences such as arts engagement shape the creative functioning of the brain, and serve as the basis for integrating the arts more effectively in early education programs and lifelong learning?

Most studies about the effects of arts education are short-term, with small sample sizes, and they use a variety of assessment methods. In the future, such research will benefit from implementing stronger study designs, including larger and more diverse study samples, and using standardized measures across a broad array of domains of children's competence.

- *Gap:* There is a need to fund longitudinal studies that track children into school and even adulthood to determine how early arts interventions may contribute to later life outcomes; there is also a need to develop standardized tools that better measure the effects of arts education and arts experiences.
- *Gap:* Procedures should be developed to help educators integrate the new research findings into their program design and instructional activities, and to help educators monitor the development of young children's creativity.

End Notes

[1] Child Welfare Information Gateway, *Understanding the Effects of Maltreatment on Brain Development*, issue brief, accessed August 16, 2011, http://www.childwelfare.gov/pubs /issue_briefs/brain_ development/how.cfm.

[2] Erik H. Erikson, Joan M. Erikson, and Helen Q. Kivnick, *Vital Involvement in Old Age* (New York: Norton, 1986).

[3] Neal S. Halfon, *Life Course Health Development: A New Approach for Addressing Upstream Determinants of Health and Spending* (Washington: Expert Voices, National Institute for

The Arts and Human Development 97

Health Care Management Foundation, 2009), accessed August 8, 2011, http://www.nihcm. org/pdf/ExpertVoices_Halfon_FINAL.pdf.

[4] Jessie White, *The Educational Ideas of Froebel* (London: University Tutorial Press, 1907), 61, accessed August 8, 2011. http://core. roehampton.ac.uk/digital/froarc/whited/

[5] Edward F. Zigler and Sandra J. Bishop-Josef. "The Cognitive Child vs the Whole Child: Lessons from 40 years of Head Start." In *Play = Learning: How Play Motivates and Enhances Children's Cognitive and Social–Emotional Growth,* eds. Dorothy G. Singer, Roberta Michnik Golinkoff, and Kathy Hirsh-Pasek. (New York: Oxford University Press, 2006), 15–35.

[6] James S. Catterall, "Research and Assessment on the Arts and Learning: Education Policy Implications of Recent Research on the Arts and Academic and Social Development," *Journal for Learning Through Music* 3 (2003): 103–109; Laura H. Chapman, "No Child Left Behind in Art?" *Arts Education Policy Review* 106 (2004): 3–17.

[7] Frances H. Rauscher, et al., "Music training causes long-term enhancement of preschool children's spatial-temporal reasoning," *Neurological Research,* 19 *(*1997): 2-8; E. Glenn Schellenberg, "Musical and Nonmusical Abilities," *Annals of the New York Academy of Sciences,* 930 (2001): 355–371.

[8] Lois Hetland, "Learning to Make Music Enhances Spatial Reasoning," *Journal of Aesthetic Education,* 34, no. 3/4 (2000): 179–238.

[9] Cybele C. Raver and Jane Knitzer, Ready to Enter: What Research Tells Policymakers About Strategies to Promote Social and Emotional School Readiness Among Three and Four-Year-Old Children (New York: National Center for Children in Poverty, Mailman School of Public Health, Columbia University, 2002).

THE ARTS IN YOUTH AND ADOLESCENCE

Adolescence represents a critical transition period that includes profound biological changes associated with puberty as well as important developmental changes such as the need to explore normative behavior and to establish increased levels of independence. Teenagers are preparing to assume greater levels of responsibility, including entering the workforce and considering building families. Their preparedness for these adult responsibilities (or lack thereof) will have a profound effect on their own happiness and well-being, and on their ability to contribute in significant ways to the vitality and stability of the larger society.

Teenagers are acutely sensitive to environmental influences. Factors such as family, peer group, school, neighborhood, policies, and societal cues can either support or challenge a teen's health and well-being. Promoting the adolescent's positive development will facilitate the adoption of healthy behaviors and help to ensure a healthy and productive future population.[1]

Research reveals that arts learning experiences can alter the attitudes of young people toward themselves and each other. Students involved in sustained theater arts (e.g., scene study, acting techniques, dramatic or musical theater production) show gains not only in reading proficiency, but also in self-control, motivation, and empathy and tolerance for others. An arts experience can promote shared purpose and the team spirit required, for example, to perform in an ensemble music group or to design and paint a community mural.

Evidence-Based Claims

The following studies exemplify the state of current evidence supporting the benefits of art and arts education for adolescents and young adults.

Arts Education, Academic Success, and Life Skills

1. Catterall, Chapleau, and Iwanaga (1999): In an article that appeared in *Champions of Change: The Impact of Arts on Arts Learning*, a publication cosponsored by the Arts Education Partnership and the President's Committee on the Arts and the Humanities, Catterall presented an analysis of data from the U.S. Department of Education's National Educational Longitudinal Survey (NELS). The study aimed at identifying relationships between arts involvement and academic performance. The researchers found that although the probability of having more arts experiences in school was greater for economically advantaged students, students with high involvement in the arts, including racial/ethnic minority and low-income groups, performed better in school and stayed in school longer than students with low arts involvement.

Some of the key differences the researchers found for math proficiency were between students highly involved in the arts and non-arts-involved students. The overall probability of scoring high in mathematics among all 12th grade students was about 21 percent. The researchers found that all students in the high socioeconomic status (SES) quartile did better than the average student, with over 38 percent scoring high in mathematics. However, high-SES students concentrating in instrumental music did substantially better than those with no involvement in music, with 48 percent scoring high. Of note, over 33 percent of low-SES students with high involvement in music scored high in mathematics—far better than the average student. Over the school years, the relative advantage of arts-involved, low-SES students also increased.

2. Winner and Hetland (2002): Harvard's Project Reap (Reviewing Education and the Arts Project) conducted a comprehensive meta-analytic

The Arts and Human Development

review of studies (1950–1999) to test the claim that arts learning causes some form of academic improvement. The research team noted that the quest for instrumental value in arts programs (i.e., that engagement in arts programs improves performance in other academic areas) is a double-edged sword. "It is implausible," wrote the authors, "to suppose that the arts can be as effective a means of teaching an academic subject as is direct teaching of that subject."

The REAP review did, however, find a number of areas suggesting causal links between arts training and improvement in other academic areas, including:

- *Classroom Drama and Verbal Skills*—Based on 80 research reports, a causal link was found between enacting drama texts and a variety of verbal areas, including oral understanding, recall of stories, reading readiness, reading achievement, oral language, and writing. Written understanding/recall of stories showed especially robust results.
- *Learning to Play Music and Spatial Reasoning*—Based on 19 reports, a "large" causal relationship was found between learning to make music and acquiring spatial-temporal reasoning skills. The effect was greater when standard music notation was learned as well.
- *Listening to Music and Spatial-Temporal Reasoning*—Based on 26 reports, a "medium"-sized causal relationship was found between listening to music and temporary improvement in spatial-temporal reasoning.
- *Dance and Visual-Spatial Skills*—Based on three research reports, a "small" to medium-sized causal relationship was found between dance and improved visual-spatial skills.

3. Catterall (2009): As a follow-up to his 1999 analysis of the U.S. Department of Education's National Educational Longitudinal Survey (NELS: 88) results, James Catterall again mined the database for arts-specific information and reported the findings in his book *Doing Well and Doing Good by Doing Art: A 12-year Longitudinal Study of Arts Education—Effects on the Achievements and Values of Young Adults.*

The NELS: 88 study tracked 25,000 secondary school students over four years and found significant connections between high involvement in the arts and general academic success. In 2009, Catterall analyzed ten additional years of data for the same cohort of students (then age 26). The study provided important empirical evidence of the role arts education can play in preparing young people for success in school and in their life beyond school years.

The study found the persistence of strong connections between arts learning from the earlier years and overall academic success and pro-social outcomes. Not only did the advantages in performance of the arts-involved students relative to other students increase over time, the arts-engaged low-income students were more likely than their non-arts-engaged peers to have attended and done well in college, obtained employment, volunteered in their communities, and participated in the political process by voting. Findings suggest that the arts' role in developing competency may be especially important for students who otherwise feel isolated or excluded.

4. Pittsburgh Public Schools (2009): The subject of this evaluation study was the Greater Arts Integration Initiative (GAIN), a collaboration between the School District of Pittsburgh and the Manchester Craftsmen's Guild (MCG) to integrate visual arts into the curriculum for grades six through eight at Faison Academy Intermediate School. GAIN received support from the U.S. Department of Education's Arts Education Model Development and Dissemination grants program.

MCG artists worked with teachers to develop and implement arts-integrated lessons for Communications, Math, World Cultures, and Science classes. Professional development workshops helped teachers become more familiar with arts-integration techniques in the classroom. In addition, a designated behavior specialist coached teachers on classroom management strategies. In the second year of the grant, MCG placed permanent artists in the school to work with teachers on arts-integrated project designs and implementation.

GAIN used a quasi-experimental design with a matched-control school for comparison. The study found that student behavior, measured by lower numbers of suspensions and discipline referrals, improved in schools involved in GAIN, as did student attendance. Students' academic achievement also improved: seventh-grade students in treatment schools significantly outperformed control-group students on the Pennsylvania State Standard Assessment (PSSA) in Reading and Math, with 23.6 percent and 20.8 percent achieving proficiency or above on each section respectively, compared to 11.8 percent of the control group for each section.

5. Israel (2009): This study examined the relationship between school-based arts education and high school graduation rates in New York City public schools. The study used data from the New York City Department of Education's "Annual Arts in Schools" reports in addition to graduation rate data. The analysis included a total of 189 New York City high schools from the 2006-07 school year and 239 from the 2007–08 school year.

The study found that schools in the top third of graduation rates offered their students the most access to arts education and the most resources that support arts education. Schools in the bottom third of graduation rates consistently offered the least access and fewest resources. This pattern held true for nine key indicators that convey a school's commitment to arts education: the presence in these schools of certified arts teachers, dedicated arts classrooms, appropriately equipped arts classrooms, arts and cultural partnerships, coursework in the arts, access to a multi-year arts sequence, school sponsorship of student arts participation, school sponsorship of arts field trips, and availability of external funds to support the arts.

In 1992, Chicago's arts and education leaders decided that if they worked together, more progress could be made on providing the city's children with access to arts education. They formed the Chicago Arts Partnerships in Education (CAPE), a partnership involving about 50 artists and arts organizations and 120 Chicago public schools. Teachers, parents, principals, artists, and arts organizations develop long-term partnerships to co-develop new solutions to enduring problems in schools and communities. These alliances serve as a living laboratory for a community of artists and teachers dedicated to infusing arts throughout the curriculum, and for a community of researchers dedicated to understanding how teaching through the arts improves student achievement. CAPE has been replicated in other cities across the United States, Canada, and England.

Chicago Arts Partnerships in Education.

Additional evidence is found in the Arts Education Partnership's second compilation of research, *Critical Links: Learning in the Arts and Student Academic and Social Development*. This publication summarized findings from 62 studies. Across five arts disciplines—dance, drama, multi-arts, music, and visual arts—the studies made claims for a variety of learning that occurred in other domains.

Arts Education- in out-of-School Settings

6. Heath (1999): This decade-long, mixed-methods study examined the daily operations of 124 youth-based organizations across the United States. Shirley Brice Heath and her team observed events ranging from program planning to evaluation. They made audio recordings of adults and young members engaging in practice, critique sessions, and celebrations. Teams of young people were also trained as ethnographers, interviewing local residents and youth not involved with youth-based organizations and supervising other young people's participation in daily logs and journals. In 1994, a sample of youth organization members responded to the U.S. Department of Education's National Education Longitudinal Survey, which allowed comparison to a national sample of high school students.

Among the findings associated with this study, Heath observed that the learning environments of arts organizations were somewhat different than those of community service or sports organizations. Students involved in after-school activities at arts organizations demonstrated greater use of complex language than might have been obtained in English or Social Studies classrooms. Heath arrived at this conclusion by comparing language that theater groups used to classroom language available in published materials. Students who were involved in arts education for at least nine hours a week were also four times more likely than their peers nationally to have won school-wide recognition for their academic achievement and three times more likely to have won an award for school attendance.

7. Larson, Hansen, and Moneta (2006): Published in *Developmental Psychology*, this article inventoried the types of developmental and self-reported negative experiences that youth encountered in different categories of extracurricular and community-based organized activities. The study's goal was to identify the average profile associated with each category. The researchers also sought to compare experiences in these activities with three other major activities in the lives of youth (school classes, leisure with friends, early job experiences) to gauge the opportunities presented by organized activities in relation to meaningful benchmarks. A representative sample of

2,280 11th-graders from 19 diverse high schools responded to a computer-administered protocol.

Students in arts activities reported significantly higher rates of experiences related to personal initiative compared to other students, but also reported lower rates for certain other experiences. Of note, the arts students reported significantly higher rates of experiences involving identity exploration, compared to other students.

8. Shernoff and Vandell (2007): This study compared the experiences of 165 middle school students at eight after-school programs that offered a variety of activities. David Jordan Shernoff and colleagues sought to discover the average levels of subjective experience measures (i.e., intrinsic motivation, concentrated effort, positive and negative mood states, and engagement) during selected activities in the after-school programs. A total of 1,596 experiences were randomly sampled using the Experience Sampling Method (ESM), which linked activities and social partners with momentary fluctuations in participants' cognitive and emotional states.

Study findings revealed high levels of engagement while participating in arts enrichment activities (e.g., dance, drama, visual arts, music). Students reported significantly higher intrinsic motivation, concentrated effort, and engagement, and lower apathy when participating in the arts, compared to being engaged in other activities. The researchers concluded that the positive experience of youth during arts enrichment activities—both in terms of intrinsic motivation and concentrated effort (a combination characteristic of positive youth engagement and development)—provides additional justification to expand research on the arts.

Looking to the Future

Youth are moving from a role as receivers of culture to creators of culture. In a 21st-century learning environment, children increasingly must know how to deal with massive amounts of information, communicate globally, and organize more of their own learning. In today's global economy, moreover, creativity and innovation are essential.

- *Gap:* Research on how new technologies affect the minds and creativity of young learners, both positively and negatively, is critical. What happens to adolescent brains when exposed to massive amounts of information?

- *Gap:* Can engagement in arts programs help adolescents gain critical thinking and metacognitive skills that will help them organize their own learning and function within the new environment of global communications?

Evidence suggests that arts education programs can have a beneficial effect on school climates, helping motivate adolescents to stay in school and often triggering their interest in other subjects.

- *Gap:* Further research is needed to pinpoint what types of arts programs are most effective in promoting academic success and pro-social behavior in adolescents.

End Notes

[1] Clea McNeely and Jayne Blanchard, *The Teen Years Explained: A Guide to Healthy Adolescent Development* (Baltimore: Johns Hopkins Bloomberg School of Public Health, Center for Adolescent Health, 2009).

THE ARTS AND OLDER ADULTS

The geriatric landscape is shifting—due, in part, to two of the most significant global phenomena of the 21st century: widespread population aging and the rapid diffusion of technology. With regard to aging, the oldest baby-boomers turn 65 in 2011. And, between 2005 and 2030, the number of adults aged 65 and older will virtually double—from 37 million to 72 million.[1]

Additionally, the number of older adults with chronic disease is on the rise. Eight out of ten older adults have one or more chronic diseases that will require coordinated and compassionate care.[2] Confronted with growing numbers of Americans who have chronic disease or dementia, U.S. policymakers, health practitioners, and the public must direct greater emphasis on finding solutions to long-term care and care-giving issues.[3] In tough fiscal times, moreover, those solutions will require highly cost-effective strategies.

As the geriatric landscape shifts to accommodate older adults, customized technology will continue to be developed in response to the challenges of aging. These opportunities likely will include new approaches to foster community-based care, health-related assessment, safety-monitoring, connectivity, lifelong learning, legacy-leaving, and adaptive environments. As the research below suggests, the arts can complement these approaches in helping to improve the quality of life for older adults.

Evidence-Based Claims

The following studies exemplify the state of current evidence supporting the benefits of art and arts education for older adults.

Arts Participation: Optimizing Health Outcomes
1. Cohen, et al. (2006): In a study co-funded by the NEA and the National Institute of Mental Health and other sponsors, Gene Cohen measured the impact of professionally conducted cultural programs on the physical health, mental health, and social functioning of older adults. Participants were 166 healthy, ambulatory, older adults from the Washington, DC area (average age: 80), who were assigned randomly either to an intervention (chorale) or comparison group (control; usual activity) and assessed at baseline and after 12 months.

Results showed positive findings of the intervention's effectiveness. The intervention group reported higher overall physical health, fewer doctor visits, less medication use, fewer instances of falls, and fewer health problems when compared to the comparison group. The intervention group also evidenced better morale and less loneliness than the comparison group. Similarly, the comparison group had a significant decline in total number of activities, whereas the intervention group reported a trend toward increased activity.

2. Houston, et al. (2011): Storytelling is emerging as a powerful tool for health promotion in vulnerable populations. For this article, which appeared in the *Annals of Internal Medicine*, Thomas Houston and colleagues performed a study to test an interactive storytelling intervention to improve blood-pressure control among African Americans. The researchers conducted a randomized, controlled trial in which 230 patients received a series of three storytelling DVDs that were delivered at baseline, three months, and six months. All of the participants had physician-diagnosed hypertension. Adults in the intervention group received the DVDs that contained the patient stories, while adults in the comparison group received an attention-control DVD covering health topics not related to hypertension.

The storytelling intervention produced substantial and significant improvements in blood pressure control for patients with baseline uncontrolled hypertension. The research suggests that storytelling is an intervention that can be used to deliver health-promotion information, particularly to vulnerable populations, and that it may be adaptable to other chronic conditions besides hypertension.

Arts Participation: Creativity, Cognition, and Aging

3. Noice, Noice, and Staines (2004): The research duo of Helga and Tony Noice investigated the effects of theatrical training on cognitive function and quality of life by using theater. Cognitive function and mental health were assessed via tests of word recall, listening tasks, problem-solving, and measures of self-esteem and psychological well-being. As reported in the *Journal of Aging and Health*, results revealed that the theater group scored significantly higher than both control groups on recall and problem-solving as well as on psychological well-being. Follow-up testing at four months after the intervention—to determine if the efforts were sustained in the theater-intervention group—revealed significant increases in word recall scores, and no significant decline in mental health measures.

4. Hackney, Kantorovich, and Earhart (2007): People with Parkinson's disease (PD) have difficulty turning while walking; turning can trigger freezing of gait. Madeline Hackney and colleagues evaluated whether the functional mobility benefits noted in older adults who had participated in a tango-dancing program might extend to adults with Parkinson's disease. Thirty-eight subjects were assigned either to a control (exercise) group or tango group in which ten one-hour-long exercise or tango classes were completed in 13 weeks.

These adults were assessed prior to training and after the ten sessions. All completed the Modified Falls Efficacy Scale, the Activities-Specific Balanced Confidence scale, and the 17-item Philadelphia Geriatric Center Morale Scale. Balance was evaluated using the functional reach and one-leg stance test. Walking velocity measurement sessions were videotaped and analyzed.

Only the PD tango group improved on all measures of balance, falls, and gait. The findings revealed that tango is an effective and feasible modality for improving mental function and balance. The study also lays the groundwork for further exploration into special features of dance and expressive movement done to a rhythmical pulse to gain functional mobility.

5. Noice and Noice (2009): In a follow-up to their 2004 study, Helga and Tony Noice sought to replicate their 2004 results with an at-risk population. Pre- and post-tests of cognitive ability were given to the experimental/intervention theater group and to two control groups (a singing group

The Arts and Human Development 107

and a no-treatment control group); 122 adults participated. The theater intervention group engaged in eight sessions held twice a week for four weeks.

Findings showed that the theater group had significant improvements compared to the two control groups in four of the five cognitive measures: immediate word recall, problem-solving, verbal fluency, and delayed recall. Noice and Noice suggest that the multimodal nature of theatrical engagement, which engages physical, cognitive, and psychosocial faculties, contributes to the positive effects of the intervention.

Imagination and Art Processes: Alzheimer's Disease and Dementia

6. Fritsch, et al. (2009): As Alzheimer's disease (AD) progresses, memory and language fade, but other parts of the mind sometimes spring to life, such as those touched by art. Thomas Fritsch and colleagues investigated the impact of a ten-week TimeSlips (TS) storytelling intervention on quality of care for persons with dementia residing in long-term-care facilities. The TimeSlips program encourages people with AD and related dementias to express themselves creatively through group-generated stories without relying on failing memories. Participants are asked open-ended questions about a dramatic picture, and responses are recorded, woven into a story, and read back to the group. Results indicated that those in the TS facilities were more engaged and more alert. There were more frequent staff-resident interactions, social interactions, and social engagement in TS facilities than in non-TS facilities. Staff in TS communities developed more positive views of people with dementia and devalued residents less than the control group did. There were no differences in job satisfaction.

7. Philips, Reid-Arndt, and Pak (2010): In a second TimeSlips study, Lorraine Philips and her research team tested the effectiveness of TimeSlips on communication, neuropsychiatric symptoms, and quality of life in long-term care residents with dementia. A quasi-experimental study design was used to compare persons with dementia in the TS intervention group with those in the usual-care group. Both groups met twice weekly for six weeks, and were tested at baseline and post-intervention at weeks seven and ten. Participants received the Cornell Scale for Depression in Dementia, the Neuropsychiatry Inventory-Nursing Home Version, the Functional Assessment of Communication Skills, the Quality of Life-Alzheimer's Disease Assessment, and the Observed Emotion Rating Scale. TimeSlips participants showed a heightened degree of pleasure and improved communication skills— effects that persisted at week seven. Celebration and play are part of the interactions in TS programs; adults who took part in TimeSlips were active participants, rather than passive recipients.

8. Rosenberg, et al. (2009): An evidence-based, nine-month study to gauge the effect of the "Meet Me at the MOMA" program was designed for people in early stages of dementia and their family caregivers. The intervention consisted of eight adults with dementia and their respective family member (usually the main caregiver). Led by a trained art educator, the tour presented art in a predetermined sequence, lasting 1.5 hours, and devoting 15–20 minutes to each artwork. Researchers selected a battery of scales that were used to capture the experience. Self-rating scales administered before and one week after the program, observer-rated scales, and a take-home evaluation were used to collect data and capture participant feedback.

Founded in 2004 in Santa Fe, New Mexico, the Alzheimer's Poetry Project (APP) has a mission to enhance the quality of life for people with Alzheimer's disease, along with their families and professional healthcare workers. APP has held 300 programming sessions at 75 facilities in Arizona, Arkansas, California, Colorado, Connecticut, Georgia, New Jersey, New Mexico, New York, Pennsylvania, Oklahoma, Texas, Virginia, and Washington, DC, serving more than 9,500 people living with Alzheimer's disease. APP also has led staff training for over 800 healthcare workers and family members in using poetry in adults with dementia. The National Endowment for the Arts supported a recent project in which poet Jimmy Santiago Baca trained local artists to facilitate poetry workshops, conducted in both Spanish and English, for individuals who have Alzheimer's disease. A culminating event, held at the National Hispanic Cultural Center, will include readings of poems created by the patients.

Alzheimer's Poetry Project.

Findings revealed statistically significant and substantively visible mood changes in both the caregiver group and the people who had dementia. Caregivers reported an enhanced sense of self-esteem. They appreciated seeing their family members treated with respect and being able to engage with them in a gracious and beautiful environment.

Building Community and Strong Social Networks

9. Gonzales, Morrow-Howell, and Gilbert (2010): The Vital Visionaries program is designed to improve medical students' attitudes toward older adults. The intergenerational group of older adults and medical students met for four two-hour sessions at art museums to create and discuss art. Three hundred and twenty-eight individuals participated: 112 medical students in the treatment group, 96 in the comparison group, and 120 older adults. The medical students completed pre- and post-surveys that captured their attitude toward older adults, perceptions of commonality with older adults, and career plans.

This evaluation study revealed that the "Vital Visionary" students became more positive in their attitudes toward older adults, and felt they had more in common with them. According to the findings of Ernest Gonzales and his research team, socializing these groups (with healthy older adults) through art can foster positive attitudes and enhance commonality with older adults. The arts provide a sense of community through sharing an activity, looking past stereotypes, using the mind, and engaging the senses.

10. Jeffri (2011): In *Still Kicking: Aging Performing Artists in NYC and LA Metro Areas*, Joan Jeffri continued the pioneering work of her research on aging artists. The study aimed to understand how artists, who often reach artistic maturity and increased artistic satisfaction as they age, are supported and integrated within their communities and how their social network structures change over time. Jeffri's hypothesis was that artists, who have learned how to adapt during their entire life course, can be a model for U.S. society as the workforce changes to accommodate multiple careers, and as baby-boomers enter retirement.

Results showed that older adults with strong networks are more likely to stay out of nursing homes and to display quality-of-life benefits, compared to adults with less diverse social networks. (Artists generally have robust social networks—a strong indicator of social capital.) The artists in the study ranked high on life- satisfaction scales and had high self-esteem as individuals and as artists. The majority reported that they will never retire from their art-making. Although self-esteem typically declines with age, over 83 percent of aging performing artists rated their self-esteem as individuals and self-esteem as artists as good to excellent.

Looking to the Future

The dramatic rise of older Americans in the general population presents both a challenge and a unique opportunity for strategic partnerships and new research agendas.

In 2009, Castora-Binkley, et al. conducted a systematic literature review to examine research publications on participatory arts programs for older adults and their reported impact on health outcomes.[4] A total of 2,205 articles were found, but only 11 were eligible for inclusion. The review revealed a paucity of research in this area. Of the studies reviewed, the researchers concluded that the most rigorous had been conducted by Cohen, et al. and the research team of Noice and Noice.

- *Gap:* There is a strong need to replicate and extend the types of studies undertaken by Cohen and the Noices in demonstrating how participation in arts programs improves health, mood, and cognition in older adults.

In older adults, arts engagement appears to encourage health-promoting behaviors (physical and mental stimulation, social engagement, self-mastery, and stress reduction) that can help prevent cognitive decline and address frailty and palliative care through strengths-based arts interventions. Prevention can have profound effects on individual quality of life and on the cost of healthcare.

- *Gap:* Further research is needed to confirm that arts engagement has these beneficial effects and to identify which kinds of arts interventions are most effective.
- *Gap:* Sophisticated cost-benefit analyses should be conducted to quantify the long-term savings that may accrue from integrating the arts into preventive and therapeutic health programs for older adults.
- *Gap:* Intergenerational arts learning offers great promise for leveraging the strengths, skills, and experiences of older adults. Studies should be conducted to identify the unique potential benefits

The Arts and Human Development

that result from programs engaging older and younger people together in arts learning as individuals, families, and community members.

End Notes

[1] Administration on Aging, U.S. Department of Health and Human Services, *A Profile of Older Americans: 2010,* accessed August 8, 2011, http://www.aoa.gov/aoaroot/aging_statistics /Profile/2010/docs/2010profile.pdf.

[2] Institute of Medicine, *Retooling for an Aging America: Building the Health Care Workforce,* accessed August 8, 2011, http://www.nap.edu/catalog.php?record_id=12089.

[3] ILC-SCSHE Taskforce, The Caregiving Project for Older Americans, *Caregiving in America* (New York: ILC-USA, 2006).

[4] Melissa Castora-Binkley, et al., "Impact of Arts Participation on Health Outcomes for Older Adults," *Journal of Aging, Humanities and the Arts* 4 (2010): 352–367.

RECOMMENDATIONS AND CONCLUSION

The research presented at the March 2011 NEA-HHS convening, and augmented in this white paper, is replete with promising findings. Studies supported by the Dana Foundation around learning, arts, and the brain underscore improvements in both cognitive and behavioral development. A growing body of research affirms the impact the arts may have on the school-readiness of young children at risk, including children from low-income and racial/ethnic minority backgrounds, and on improved academic and behavioral outcomes in youth. Research into the impact of arts learning and engagement has also revealed a host of beneficial health, cognitive, and social outcomes for older adults. Although the research results are promising, the majority of the studies cited here have design limitations such as relatively small, non-diverse samples and non-com-parable outcome measures. Larger, more robust studies across the sectors of health and human services are warranted to enlarge an evidence-based body of knowledge sufficient to justify broad-based policy changes and best-practices replication. Forum participants agreed that a collective leap forward must be taken to address the challenges of building an evidence base. In particular, the following challenges remain:

- *A lack of coordination* among federal agency departments and investigators and practitioners from various disciplines (e.g., arts education, child development, geriatrics, nursing, educational

112   Gay Hanna, Michael Patterson, Judy Rollins et al.

psychology, cognitive neuroscience, the behavioral and social sciences) in pursuing a vigorous research agenda to understand the role of arts and arts education in human development.

- *The small size of study populations* participating in research on the arts and human development currently limits generalizability of the results. So far, the majority of reported studies rely on correlational data, rather than results from well-controlled trials. Another limiting factor is the dearth of longitudinal studies.
- *Low visibility of research findings*, program evaluation data, and evidence-based models integrating the arts in health and educational programs that occur for various segments of the lifespan.

These needs have acquired greater currency in light of recent demographic trends and domestic policy priorities. With an increasingly diverse population, a rising cohort of highly active baby-boomers facing retirement, and larger numbers of older adults with chronic diseases, opportunities for creative engagement and lifelong learning in the arts are likely to prove critical for greater health and well-being. Education leaders and communities, confronted with large percentages of Americans failing to finish high school, are seeking innovative and effective strategies to engage students and boost their achievement levels. In this climate, a stronger role for arts education should be investigated. Finally, the high-order critical thinking and creativity skills that have been linked to arts training are deemed increasingly vital to today's workforce, to the U.S. economy, and to overall competitiveness. At the NEA-HHS event, Mary Wright, a program director with the Conference Board, summarized findings from several industry surveys of employers: "Creativity and innovation are going to increase in importance." Likewise, educators increasingly recognize that creativity is a key competency to be developed in school and is applicable to all subject areas. According to U.S. Secretary of Education Arne Duncan, the most effective way to foster creativity is through arts education.[1]

Recommendations

The moment is ripe for federal leadership in the design, conduct, and dissemination of rigorous research and evidence-based practices documenting the arts' contributions to human development—from early childhood, adolescence, and young adulthood to middle-aged and older adults.

The Arts and Human Development 113

Participants at the NEA-HHS event on March 14, 2011, included representatives from federal agencies as well as from the private and not-for-profit sectors of national, state, and local service organizations representing the arts, health, education, and social services. Each area of government represented, in partnership with supporting organizations, has the potential to establish joint initiatives to better serve in the promotion of health and wellness across the life-span through arts learning and participation. With additional communication and coordination between key agencies, resources could be shared broadly across the federal government. Common policy goals and coordinated, inter-agency strategies would promote effective outcomes and more efficient use of resources.

To support this leadership role, the following actions are recommended:

1. Establish a federal interagency task force to promote the regular sharing of research and information about the arts and human development.

The task force would include high-level officials from the National Endowment for the Arts, the Department of Education, and HHS agencies such as the Administration for Children and Families, the Administration on Aging, and the National Institutes of Health. The group would convene two to three times a year to review progress on the following tasks:

- *Host a series of webinars* spotlighting examples of compelling research and evidence-based practices that have integrated the arts in human development. The webinars will be aimed at the public, but especially at researchers and providers of the arts, health, and education for various segments of the lifespan.
- *Coordinate the distribution of information* about funding opportunities for researchers and providers of the arts, health, and education across the lifespan.
- *Conduct or commission an inventory and gap analysis* of federally sponsored research on the arts and human development so that future research opportunities can be developed by and across agencies, departments, and the private sector.
- *Develop an online clearinghouse* of research and evidence-based practices that examine or utilize the arts in health and educational programs across the lifespan.

2. Convene a series of technical workshops to help develop strong research proposals that represent robust and innovative study design and methods to investigate the relationship between the arts and human development.

If the most competitive research proposals are to reach the appropriate funders, then capacity-building through peer learning must occur. A series of workshops would help to improve the overall rigor of such studies, by recruiting outstanding scientists to tackle vexing and complex problems in pursuing this topic.

Because of formidable difficulties involved in mounting large-scale, longitudinal studies of the arts at work in human development—and because of the complexity of study design factors related to different age populations—it is important to bring together research methodologists and content experts in neuroscience, health, education, and the arts to advance discussion of key topics, including:

- *What are appropriate outcomes* (including quality-of-life indicators) for studies comparing arts interventions with control groups in the provision of health and/or educational services?
- *How might successful randomization be achieved* and comparison study design models developed for exploring the arts' potential impact, particularly on children and older adults?
- *How can diversity in the study populations be promoted* to ensure that findings about the arts and human development will apply toward and thus benefit all groups (e.g., individuals from all ages and different racial/ethnic backgrounds, including those with disabilities)?
- *How can artists and arts educators contribute fully* to the planning and conduct of research? What protocols and criteria should guide the administration of arts content and delivery?

3. Bring the arts to national and inter-national conversations about integrating the concept of well-being into policy development.

Even while new evidence is being gathered, the federal partnership should leverage growing national and international interest in using measures of subjective well-being as complementary and valuable tools to guide policy decisions. This discussion is highly consistent with the HHS strategic goal— "Advance the health, safety, and well-being of the American people." At the same time, greater analysis of the arts in direct relationship to well-being will provide the NEA with an opportunity to realize one of its own goals for the American people—"Promote public knowledge and understanding about the contribution of the arts."

The Arts and Human Development 115

This recommendation also aligns with two National Institute on Aging-sponsored efforts to advance the measurement of subjective well-being for application to research on aging and health. Those efforts include:

- Development of a National Research Council panel on "measuring subjective well-being in a policy-relevant framework." This initiative, cosponsored by the UK Economic and Social Research Council, was singled out by the White House in a May 25, 2011, joint fact sheet as having "the potential to generate new insights that will directly inform social and economic policies."
- A series of National Academies of Sciences workshops that will conclude in September 2012 with recommendations on the "evaluation of measures of subjective well-being and development of OECD guidance for national statistical agencies on the measurement of well-being." The workshops should be monitored for their potential applicability to future federal data collection about the arts' role in human development.

Conclusion

At the outset of the NEA-HHS convening on March 14, 2011, NEA Chairman Landesman declared: "The arts are central to human development. Movement, song, rhythm, and storytelling are the earliest ways that babies and their families interact, and these are the same impulses that stay with us over our entire lives."

The NEA chairman reinforced the primal connection between the arts and human development.

"We know all this experientially," Landesman said. "Anyone who has sung a lullaby or danced a child to sleep or listened to a young person's imaginative adventures has witnessed this." He urged the forum's participants to "take the anecdotal and turn it into a framework for the NEA and HHS to work together."

HHS Secretary Sebelius equally supported the call for action. "We strongly believe that the arts can inspire and move people to do great things," she said, noting that "our department has stressed the role of arts in health from day one."

"Therefore," the HHS secretary added, "we hope this meeting leads to deeper collaboration in research and in identifying new ways to engage the arts to improve people's lives."

True to its purpose, "The Arts and Human Development: Learning across the Lifespan" convening has resulted in the framework for long-term collaboration among the NEA, HHS, and other federal agencies to build capacity for future research and evidence-sharing about the role of the arts in human development. The additional research made possible through collaboration will lead to effective, replicable models for improving quality of life and related outcomes through the arts, for Americans at different stages of their lives. Based on the findings of the NEA-HHS convening and white paper, there could be no better time to take existing research on the arts and human development to the next crucial phase.

REFERENCES

Administration on Aging, U.S. Department of Health and Human Services. *A Profile of Older Americans: 2010.* Accessed August 8, 2011. *http://www.aoa.gov/aoaroot/aging_statistics/Profile/2010/docs/2010profil e.pdf*

Asbury, Carolyn and Barbara Rich, eds. *Learning, Arts, and the Brain: The Dana Consortium Report on Arts and Cognition.* Organized by Michael Gazzaniga. New York/Washington, DC: Dana Press, 2008.

Berkowitz, Aaron L., and Daniel Ansari. "Generation of Novel Motor Sequences: The Neural Correlates of Musical Improvisation." *NeuroImage* 41, no. 2 (2008): 535–543.

Brown, Eleanor D., Barbara Benedett, and M. Elizabeth Armistead. "Arts Enrichment and School Readiness for Children at Risk." *Early Childhood Research Quarterly* 25 (2010): 112–124.

Bronson, Po, and Ashley Merryman. "The Creativity Crisis." *Newsweek.* July 10, 2010. Accessed August 8, 2011. *http://www.thedailybeast.com /newsweek/2010/07/10/ the-creativity-crisis.html.*

Castora-Binkley, Melissa, Linda Noelker, Thomas Prohaska, and William Satariano. "Impact of Arts Participation on Health Outcomes for Older Adults." *Journal of Aging, Humanities and the Arts* 4 (2010): 352–367.

Catterall, James S. *Doing Well and Doing Good by Doing Art: A 12-year Longitudinal Study of Arts Education—Effects on the Achievements and Values of Young Adults.* Los Angeles: I-Group Books, 2009.

Catterall, James S. "Research and Assessment on the Arts and Learning: Education Policy Implications of Recent Research on the Arts and Academic and Social Development." *Journal for Learning Through Music* 3 (2003): 103–109.

Catterall, James S., Richard Chapleau, and John Iwanaga. "Involvement in the Arts and Human Development: General Involvement and Intensive Involvement in Music and Theater Arts." In Fiske, *Champions of Change: The Impact of the Arts on Learning*, 1–18.

Chapman, Laura H. "No Child Left Behind in Art?" *Arts Education Policy Review* 106 (2004): 3–17.

Child Welfare Information Gateway. *Understanding the Effects of Maltreatment on Brain Development.* Issue brief. Accessed August 16, 2011. *http://www.childwelfare.gov/ pubs/issue_briefs/brain_development /how.cfm.*

Cohen, Gene D., Susan Perlstein, Jeff Chapline, Jeanne Kelly, Kimberly Firth, and Samuel Simmens. "The Impact of Professionally Conducted Cultural Programs on the Physical Health, Mental Health and Social Functioning of Older Adults." *The Gerontologist* 46, no. 6 (2006): 726–734.

Duncan, Arne. Foreword to *Reinvesting in Arts Education: Winning America's Future through Creative Schools.* Washington, DC: The President's Committee on the Arts and the Humanities, 2011.

Erikson, Erik H., Joan M. Erikson, and Helen Q. Kivnick. *Vital Involvement in Old Age.* New York: Norton, 1986.

Fiske, Edward B., ed. *Champions of Change: The Impact of the Arts on Learning.* Washington, DC: The Arts Education Partnership and The President's Committee on the Arts and the Humanities, 1999.

Fritsch, Thomas, Jung Kwak, Stacey Grant, Josh Lang, Rhonda R. Montgomery, and Anne D. Basting. "Impact of TimeSlips, a Creative Expression Intervention Program, on Nursing Home Residents with Dementia and Their Caregivers." *The Gerontologist*, 49, no. 1 (2009): 117–127.

Gardner, Howard. *Frames of Mind.* New York: Basic Books, Inc., 1983.

Gazzaniga, Michael. "Arts and Cognition: Finding Hints in Relationships." In Asbury and Rich, *Learning, Arts, and the Brain*, v.

Gazzaniga, Michael S. "Music, Science and the Art of Living." Panel discussion at "The Arts and Human Development: Learning across the Lifespan," a convening by the National Endowment for the Arts in partnership with the U.S. Department of Health and Human Services, Washington, DC, March 2011.

Gonzales, Ernest, Nancy Morrow-Howell, and Pat Gilbert. "Changing Medical Students' Attitudes Towards Older Adults." *Gerontology and Geriatrics Education*, 31, no. 3 (2010): 220–234.

Hackney, Madeleine E., Svetlana Kantorovich, and Gammon M. Earhart. "A Study on the Effects of Argentine Tango as a Form of Partnered Dance for those with Parkinson Disease and the Healthy Elderly." *American Journal of Dance Therapy*, 29, no. 2 (2007): 109–127.

Halfon, Neal S. *Life Course Health Development: A New Approach for Addressing Upstream Determinants of Health and Spending.* Washington: Expert Voices, National Institute for Health Care Management Foundation, 2009. Accessed August 8, 2011. http://www.nihcm.org /pdf/ExpertVoices_Halfon_FINAL.pdf.

Heath, Shirley Brice. "Imaginative Actuality: Learning in the Arts during Nonschool Hours." In Fiske, *Champions of Change: The Impact of the Arts on Learning,* 19–34.

Hetland, Lois. "Learning to Make Music Enhances Spatial Reasoning." *Journal of Aesthetic Education,* 34, no. 3/4 (2000): 179–238.

Houston, Thomas, Jeroan J. Allison, Marc Sussman, Wendy Horn, Cheryl L. Holt, John Trobaugh, Marible Salas, Maria Pisu, Yendelela L. Cuffee, Damien Larkin, Sharina D. Person, Bruce Barton, Catarina I. Kiefe, and Sandral Hullett. "Culturally Appropriate Storytelling to Improve Blood Pressure." *Annals of Internal Medicine* 54, no. 2 (2011): 77–88.

ILC-SCSHE Taskforce, The Caregiving Project for Older Americans. *Caregiving in America.* New York: ILC-USA, 2006.

Institute of Medicine. *Retooling for an Aging America: Building the Health Care Workforce,* 2008. Accessed August 8, 2011. http://www.nap.edu /catalog.php?record_id=12089.

Israel, Douglas. *Staying in School: Arts Education and New York City Graduation Rates.* New York: The Center for Arts Education, 2009.

Jeffri, Joan. Executive Summary of *Still Kicking: Aging Performing Artists in NYC and LA Metro Areas: Information on Artists IV*. New York: Research Center for Arts and Culture, 2011.

Larson, Reed W., David M. Hansen, and Giovanni Moneta. "Differing Profiles of Developmental Experiences Across Types of Organized Youth Activities." *Developmental Psychology* 42, no. 5 (2006): 849–863.

McNeely, Clea, and Jayne Blanchard. *The Teen Years Explained: A Guide to Healthy Adolescent Development.* Baltimore: Johns Hopkins Bloomberg School of Public Health, Center for Adolescent Health, 2009.

Moore, Kristin Anderson, Jacinta Bronte-Tinkew, and Ashleigh Collins. "Practices to Foster in Out-of-School Time Programs." *Research-to-Results* 2 (2010): 1–6.

Neville, Helen, Annika Andersson, Olivia Bagdade, Ted Bell, Jeff Currin, Jessica Fanning, Scott Klein, Brittni Lauinger, Eric Pakulak, David Paulsen, Laura Sabourin, Courtney Stevens, Stephanie Sundborg, and Yoshiko Yamada. "Effects of Music Training on Brain and Cognitive Development in Under-Privileged 3- to 5-Year-Old Children: Preliminary Results." In Asbury and Rich, *Learning, Arts, and the Brain*, 105–116.

Noice, Helga, and Tony Noice. "An Arts Intervention for Older Adults Living in Subsidized Retirement Homes." *Aging, Neuropsychology and Cognition* 16, no. 1 (2009): 56–79.

Noice, Helga, Tony Noice, and Graham Staines. "A Short-Term Intervention to Enhance Cognitive and Affective Functioning in Older Adults." *Journal of Aging and Health* 16, no. 4 (2004): 562–585.

Pittsburgh Public Schools. "Profile of the Greater Arts Integration Initiative." In *Arts Model and Development and Dissemination Grants Program: 2005 Cohort Profiles,* Washington, DC: U.S. Department of Education, 1–4, ca. 2008. Accessed July 21, 2011, http://www2.ed.gov/programs/artsedmodel/performance.html.

Philips, Lorraine, Stephanie A. Reid-Arndt, and Youngju Pak. "Effects of a Creative Expression Intervention on Emotions, Communication, and Quality of Life in Persons with Dementia." *Nursing Research* 59, no. 6 (2010): 417–425.

President's Committee on the Arts and the Humanities (PCAH). *Reinvesting in Arts Education: Winning America's Future Through Creative Schools.* Washington, DC: PCAH, 2011.

Rauscher, Frances H., G.L. Shaw, L.J. Levine, E.L. Wright, W.R. Dennis, and R.L. Newcomb. "Music Training Causes Long-Term Enhancement of Preschool Children's Spatial-Temporal Reasoning." *Neurological Research,* 19 (1997): 2–8.

Raver, Cybele C., and Jane Knitzer. *Ready to Enter: What Research Tells Policymakers About Strategies to Promote Social and Emotional School Readiness Among Three and Four-YearOld Children.* New York: National Center for Children in Poverty, Mailman School of Public Health, Columbia University, 2002.

Rosenberg, Francesca, Amir Parsa, Laurel Humble, and Carrie McGee. *Meet Me: Making Art Accessible to People with Dementia.* New York: Museum of Modern Art, 2009.

Schellenberg, E. Glenn. "Musical and Nonmusical Abilities." *Annals of the New York Academy of Sciences* 930 (2001): 355–371.

Shernoff, David Jordan and Deborah Lowe Vandell. "Engagement in After-School Activities: Quality of Experience from the Perspective of Participants." *Journal of Youth Adolescence* 36, no. 7 (2007): 891–903.

Social Dynamics, LLC. "Executive summary." 2005. Evaluation report. Accessed August 8, 2011. *http:// www.socialdynamicsllc.com/completed studies.html.*

Spelke, Elizabeth. "Effects of Music Instruction on Developing Cognitive Systems at the Foundations of Mathematics and Science." In Asbury and Rich, *Learning, Arts, and the Brain*, 17–49.

White, Jessie. *The Educational Ideas of Froebel.* London: University Tutorial Press, 1907. Accessed August 8, 2011. *http://core.roehampton.ac.uk/digital/froarc/whited/.*

Winner, Ellen and Lois Hetland. "The Arts and Academic Achievement: What the Evidence Shows." *Journal of Aesthetic Education* 34, no. 3/4 (Fall/Winter 2002): 3–6.

Zigler, Edward F., and Sandra J. Bishop-Josef. "The Cognitive Child vs the Whole Child: Lessons from 40 years of Head Start." In *Play = Learning: How Play Motivates and Enhances Children's Cognitive and Social–Emotional Growth,* eds. Dorothy G. Singer, Roberta Michnik Golinkoff, and Kathy Hirsh-Pasek. New York: Oxford University Press, 2006, 15–35.

INDEX

#

21st century, ix, 81, 88, 104

A

academic performance, 89, 98
academic success, 99, 100, 104
access, 20, 22, 36, 40, 46, 49, 50, 60, 64, 101
ACF, 82
activism, 15
adjustment, 55
Administration for Children and Families, 82, 86, 113
adolescents, 54, 90, 91, 98, 104
adult education, 23
adulthood, ix, 54, 68, 82, 86, 89, 96, 112
adults, ix, 28, 38, 42, 43, 44, 82, 84, 86, 87, 91, 102, 104, 105, 106, 107, 108, 109, 110, 111, 112, 114
aesthetic, 28, 29, 34
African Americans, 105
age, 51, 87, 91, 99, 105, 109, 114
agencies, 27, 40, 41, 43, 44, 49, 50, 82, 83, 86, 88, 113, 115, 116
apathy, 103
appetite, 35

aptitude, 7
arts ecosystem, 4, 37, 46
assessment, 42, 46, 57, 58, 61, 63, 70, 96, 104
assessment tools, 42
at-risk populations, 52
attachment, 92
attitudes, 15, 35, 97, 109
awareness, 93

B

base, 111
behaviors, 42, 55, 92, 97
benchmarks, 102
beneficial effect, 104, 110
benefits, 5, 6, 7, 8, 12, 13, 15, 19, 20, 27, 28, 30, 31, 32, 34, 36, 37, 39, 40, 56, 57, 62, 66, 68, 69, 71, 91, 92, 93, 95, 98, 105, 106, 109
blood, 105
blood pressure, 105
blueprint, 3, 51
brain, 89, 91, 94, 96, 111, 117
brain functioning, 96
Bureau of Labor Statistics, 50, 61, 63, 65, 67, 74, 76, 79, 80
businesses, 7, 31, 55, 62, 75
buyer, 6

C

caliber, 18
caregivers, 108
case studies, 43, 60, 61, 66, 70, 72
catalyst, 48
causal inference, 39
causal relationship, 55, 56, 99
Census, 24, 25, 38, 41, 42, 50, 53, 58, 62, 63, 64, 65, 72, 73, 75, 76, 79, 80
challenges, 5, 22, 23, 25, 28, 30, 32, 33, 40, 49, 85, 104, 111
Chamber of Commerce, 77
Chicago, 54, 101
child development, 29, 85, 92, 111
childhood, ix, 23, 42, 44, 68, 82, 86, 89, 91, 92, 112
children, ix, 28, 42, 44, 52, 62, 67, 68, 82, 83, 87, 90, 92, 93, 94, 95, 96, 101, 103, 111, 114
chronic diseases, 104, 112
cities, 16, 55, 57, 60, 101
citizens, 9
civic engagement, 6, 39, 53, 54, 62, 68
civilization, 88
classes, 22, 23, 73, 75, 93, 94, 95, 100, 102, 106
classification, 61, 65, 74, 76
classroom, 92, 100, 102
classroom management, 100
climate, 56, 85, 112
climate change, 56
climates, 61
clustering, 53
cognition, 89, 95, 110
cognitive abilities, 95
cognitive ability, 50, 106
cognitive development, ix, 82, 92, 94
cognitive domains, 93
cognitive function, ix, 82, 106
cognitive science, 29
cognitive skills, 92, 95
collaboration, 82, 83, 100, 116

colleges, 23
commerce, 3
commercial, 4, 13, 15, 49, 50, 62, 74
communication, 48, 107, 113
communication skills, 107
community(ies), 3, 4, 5, 6, 7, 8, 9, 10, 11, 13, 14, 15, 16, 17, 19, 21, 27, 30, 33, 34, 35, 36, 40, 45, 48, 49, 54, 55, 56, 57, 58, 60, 61, 66, 69, 70, 71, 72, 73, 75, 76, 84, 85, 98, 100, 101, 102, 104, 107, 109, 111, 112
community service, 102
comparative analysis, 55
compensation, 45
competitiveness, 85, 112
compilation, 102
complement, 54, 105
complex interactions, 56
complexity, 3, 11, 16, 87, 114
composition, 16
computer, 93, 103
confidentiality, 49
Congress, vii, 1, 58
connectivity, 105
consensus, 35, 49
conservatory learning, 23
construction, 31, 54
consultation process, 4, 10
consulting, 9, 62
consumer expenditure, 67, 74
consumption, 12, 20, 23, 25
control group, 83, 84, 87, 94, 95, 100, 106, 107, 114
controlled trials, 85, 112
controversies, 8
conversations, 56, 87, 114
coordination, 85, 111, 113
correlations, 48, 55
cost, 22, 50, 88, 104, 110
covering, 105
craftsmen, 100
creative functioning, 96
creative process, 32, 96

Index

creative thinking, 35, 57, 96

creativity, viii, 7, 11, 19, 33, 36, 44, 46, 48, 50, 58, 81, 85, 86, 90, 91, 96, 103, 112, 116

criminal behavior, 52

critical thinking, 32, 53, 85, 86, 95, 104, 112

critical value, 14

criticism, 23

crowds, 27

cues, 97

cultivation, 40

culture, viii, 2, 6, 36, 55, 56, 60, 63, 65, 67, 68, 69, 71, 72, 73, 103

currency, 85, 112

curricula, 94

curriculum, 100, 101

D

dance, 53, 63, 65, 68, 69, 93, 99, 102, 103, 106

data collection, 3, 40, 46, 50, 52, 88, 115

data set, 5, 60, 66, 72, 79, 80

database, 53, 99

deficiency, 88

deficit, 39

delinquency, 55

dementia, 104, 107, 108, 109

demographic characteristics, 62

demographic data, 63, 68, 70

Department of Commerce, 39, 45

Department of Education, 42, 44, 51, 86, 98, 99, 100, 102, 113, 119

Department of Health and Human Services, 51, 57, 82, 91, 111, 116, 117

Department of Labor, 44, 50

depth, vii, viii, 2, 17

designers, 54

developmental change, 97

developmental milestones, 92

diabetes, 5

dialogues, vii, viii, 2

diffusion, 104

disability, 32, 92, 95

disposable income, 16

disposition, 28

dissonance, 49

distribution, 22, 86, 113

diversity, 6, 55, 58, 67, 69, 70, 73, 87, 114

domestic policy, 85, 112

donations, 31

dosage, 95

drawing, 36

dynamic systems, 5

E

earnings, 60, 64

economic activity, 6, 31

economic development, 31, 60, 61, 67, 69, 70, 73

economic growth, 58, 75

economic policy, 52

economic well-being, 53

economics, 4, 27, 31

ecosystem, 4, 37, 46

education, ix, 7, 11, 12, 22, 23, 36, 38, 40, 42, 44, 53, 62, 63, 65, 66, 67, 68, 70, 74, 81, 82, 84, 85, 86, 87, 88, 90, 91, 92, 93, 96, 98, 99, 100, 101, 102, 104, 105, 111, 112, 113, 114

education/training, 40

educational experience, 23

educational programs, ix, 82, 85, 86, 112, 113

educational psychology, 85, 112

educational services, 87, 114

educators, 42, 87, 96, 112, 114

elaboration, 19

emigration, 16

emotional state, 103

emotional well-being, 63, 65, 68, 69

empathy, 98

employees, 62, 75

124 Index

employers, 85, 112
employment, 25, 41, 45, 61, 62, 63, 64,
  65, 67, 73, 74, 75, 76, 84, 100
energy, 35
England, 72, 101
environment, 104, 109
environmental influences, 96, 97
Environmental Protection Agency, 44, 51
environmental stress, 92
environments, 36, 56, 105
equality, 70, 73
equipment, 20
equity, 57
ethnic background, 83, 87, 114
ethnic minority, 98, 111
ethnicity, 95
ethnographers, 102
everyday life, 56
evidence, ix, 37, 50, 56, 75, 82, 83, 84,
  85, 86, 87, 88, 90, 92, 93, 95, 98, 99,
  102, 105, 108, 111, 112, 113, 114, 116
evidence-based program, 82
evolution, 3
evolution of economies, 3
exclusion, 13
exercise, 7, 9, 36, 89, 106
expenditures, 56
experimental design, 95, 100
expertise, viii, 2, 51
exposure, 22, 32, 38, 44, 54, 89
extracts, 79, 80

F

Facebook, 14
factor analysis, 54
fairness, 57
families, 44, 83, 97, 108, 111, 115
family members, 108, 109
federal agency, 85, 111
federal government, 113
fiber, 90
financial, 7, 14, 20, 26, 27, 56

financial support, 7, 20
fitness, 89
fluctuations, 103
fMRI, 90
food, 7, 26
force, 12, 64, 86, 113
foundations, 7
freedom, 7, 11, 14, 35
freezing, 106
funding, 7, 15, 43, 44, 46, 53, 86, 113
fundraising, 20
funds, 101

G

gait, 89, 106
GDP, 47, 73
general intelligence, 95
generalizability, 85, 112
generativity, 35
geography, 6
geometry, 90
Georgia, 53, 54, 108
gifted, 51
global communications, 104
global economy, 103
grades, 100
grants, 7, 43, 46, 50, 51, 52, 58, 100
Gross Domestic Product, 39, 45, 56
growth, 6, 7, 27, 39, 45, 49, 58, 75, 91, 92
growth theory, 45
guidance, 88, 115

H

happiness, 8, 89, 97
health, viii, ix, 4, 8, 20, 43, 44, 51, 60, 63,
  64, 68, 70, 81, 82, 84, 85, 86, 87, 88,
  91, 92, 97, 104, 105, 106, 110, 111,
  112, 113, 114, 115
health insurance, 20, 60, 64
health practitioners, 104

health problems, 84, 105
health promotion, 105
health-promoting behaviors, 110
heterogeneity, 13
HHS, 82, 83, 86, 87, 88, 89, 90, 111, 112, 113, 114, 115, 116
high school, 85, 100, 102, 103, 112
hiring, 85
historical data, 47
history, 3, 6, 35, 40, 88
homogeneity, 32, 33
hospitality, 13, 27
host, 4, 111
hotel, 7
hotels, 27
housing, 60, 65, 70, 72, 75, 76
Housing and Urban Development (HUD), 45, 51, 72
human, ix, 5, 7, 8, 16, 19, 35, 43, 48, 58, 68, 75, 82, 83, 85, 86, 87, 88, 89, 91, 111, 112, 113, 114, 115, 116
human brain, 91
human capital, 58, 75
human development, ix, 43, 68, 82, 83, 85, 86, 87, 88, 89, 91, 112, 113, 114, 115, 116
human nature, 7
human resources, 7
hypertension, 105, 106
hypothesis, vii, viii, 2, 6, 54, 109

indirect effect, 27
individuality, 58
individuals, viii, ix, 3, 5, 7, 8, 9, 10, 11, 13, 14, 17, 25, 28, 29, 36, 55, 58, 74, 77, 81, 82, 83, 87, 89, 90, 108, 109, 111, 114
industry(ies), 5, 6, 13, 27, 31, 39, 40, 41, 45, 47, 52, 58, 62, 67, 74, 75, 85, 112
infrastructure, 7, 11, 20, 21, 22, 36, 40, 53, 63, 76
injury, 92, 95
institutions, 12, 20, 53
instructional activities, 96
instrumental music, 98
integration, ix, 82, 83, 84, 94, 100
intelligence, 89
intervention, 52, 84, 105, 106, 107, 108
intrinsic motivation, 103
intrinsic value, 69, 71, 74
investment, 44
investments, 40, 41, 43, 49, 73
isolation, 3, 34
Israel, 100, 118
issues, 5, 23, 25, 35, 40, 49, 60, 64, 69, 71, 74, 104

J

job creation, 27
job satisfaction, 107
Jordan, 103, 120
justification, 103
juvenile delinquency, 89

I

ideal (s), 13, 29, 32, 33, 50, 57
identification, 94
identity, 6, 67, 69, 70, 73, 103
immigration, 16
improvements, ix, 82, 95, 105, 107, 111
impulses, 115
income, 6, 13, 16, 26, 27, 57, 61, 63, 64, 65, 67, 68, 69, 70, 73, 74, 83, 84, 98, 100, 111
independence, 97

K

kindergarten, 92

L

LA Metro, 60, 64, 109, 118
labor force, 64

Index

labor market, 62, 64, 68
landscape, 104
language development, 83, 92
later life, 96
lead, 6, 7, 48, 57, 116
leadership, 58, 86, 112, 113
learners, 83, 103
learning, ix, 4, 22, 23, 50, 53, 62, 66, 81,
    82, 87, 89, 90, 92, 93, 94, 95, 97, 99,
    100, 102, 103, 104, 110, 111, 113, 114
learning environment, 102, 103
learning styles, 22
leisure, 102
liberty, 14
librarians, 43
life course, 109
life experiences, 14
lifelong learning, 85, 96, 105, 112
light, 17, 42, 85, 112
literacy, 38, 83, 93
livable communities, 51
local community, 45
local government, 57
loneliness, 84, 105
longitudinal study, 44

M

magnetic resonance imaging, 90
magnitude, 11, 94
majority, 39, 85, 109, 111, 112
mapping, 3, 11, 55, 56
Maryland, 54
mass, 15
mass media, 15
materials, 7, 14, 20, 67, 74, 102
mathematics, 83, 98
matter, 14, 21, 29
measurement(s), vii, viii, 2, 3, 4, 5, 9, 17,
    18, 20, 22, 23, 24, 27, 28, 29, 32, 34,
    35, 39, 45, 48, 49, 57, 63, 65, 67, 69,
    70, 73, 76, 88, 89, 106, 115
media, 4, 15, 16, 63, 65, 66, 67

medical, 109
medication, 84, 89, 105
medicine, 85
membership, 63, 65, 68, 69
memory, 107
mental health, 52, 105, 106
meta-analysis, 53
metacognitive skills, 95, 104
methodology, 25, 46
metropolitan areas, 31, 33
Mexico, 108
mission, 43, 83, 108
models, 12, 23, 28, 45, 49, 57, 83, 85, 88,
    112, 114, 116
mood change, 109
morale, 84, 105
mosaic, 54
motivation, 10, 12, 98, 103
motor skills, 92
multiplier, 16
multivariate analysis, 54
murals, 54
museums, 20, 109
music, 27, 44, 50, 52, 63, 65, 67, 68, 69,
    83, 90, 92, 93, 94, 95, 98, 99, 102, 103
musicians, 65, 90
mythology, 22

N

National Academy of Sciences (NAS),
    43, 51
National Institute of Mental Health, 105
National Institutes of Health, 43, 44, 51,
    82, 86, 91, 113
National Research Council, 51, 88, 91,
    115
National Survey, 55, 62
negative experiences, 102
negative mood, 103
neighborhood characteristics, 53
neurobiology, 36

neuroscience, 3, 4, 85, 87, 89, 90, 112, 114
neutral, 26
New England, 52, 72
new media, 14
New Zealand, 57, 67, 69, 70, 73
No Child Left Behind, 97, 117
nodes, 18, 19, 35, 36, 39, 41, 43, 46, 47, 48, 52
nonprofit organizations, 55
normative behavior, 97
North America, 89
NSSE, 62
nursing, 85, 109, 111
nursing home, 109

O

OECD, 88, 115
Office of Management and Budget, vii, 1, 58
officials, 82, 86, 113
Oklahoma, 108
openness, 6
operations, 102
opportunities, viii, 2, 44, 46, 49, 57, 61, 71, 85, 86, 102, 104, 112, 113
organ, viii, 2
organize, 3, 103, 104
overlap, 21, 25, 31, 33

P

palliative, 110
parents, 101
participants, viii, 2, 4, 10, 32, 54, 77, 83, 85, 103, 105, 107, 111, 115
patents, 58
pathways, ix, 82, 91, 92
payroll, 62, 75
peer group, 97
performance measurement, 58

performing artists, 60, 64, 110
Philadelphia, 72, 93, 106
physical health, 84, 105
physical sciences, 56
piano, 93
platform, 17, 49
playing, 63, 65, 68, 69
pleasure, 107
poetry, 108
policy, viii, ix, 2, 3, 5, 7, 9, 14, 16, 42, 49, 56, 81, 82, 87, 88, 91, 111, 113, 114, 115
policy options, 56
policymakers, 52, 55, 91
pollination, 15, 16
population, 11, 16, 36, 40, 44, 97, 104, 106, 110, 112
population density, 36
portfolio, 9, 46, 58
positive attitudes, 109
positive relationship, 90
potential benefits, 111
poverty, 70, 73
preparedness, 97
preschool, 83, 90, 93, 94, 95, 97
preschool children, 90, 97
President, 77, 78, 79, 98, 117, 119
primary function, 20
principles, vii, viii, 1, 2
private benefits, 69, 71, 74
private sector, 86, 113
probability, 98
problem-solving, 15, 84, 106, 107
professionals, 58
profit, 4, 39, 40, 41, 49, 64, 113
programming, 20, 52, 108
project, 4, 5, 8, 11, 37, 40, 41, 47, 48, 52, 53, 56, 59, 76, 100, 108
promoter, 13, 29
prosperity, 8, 56
psychological illnesses, 44
psychological well-being, 106
psychologist, 89, 90

128   Index

psychology, 112
puberty, 97
public goods, 71
public health, 3, 5
public policy, 52, 55
public schools, 42, 100, 101
public-private partnerships, 50
publishing, 11, 15

Q

qualitative research, 37, 54
quality of life, viii, ix, 4, 5, 6, 7, 8, 9, 15,
   36, 46, 51, 53, 55, 56, 81, 82, 83, 88,
   105, 106, 107, 108, 110, 116
quality standards, 50
quartile, 98
questionnaire, 42

R

race, 95
radio, 11
rating scale, 108
reading, 38, 63, 65, 67, 84, 98, 99
real estate, 6, 13, 57
reasoning, 90, 93, 94, 97, 99
reasoning skills, 99
recall, 84, 99, 106, 107
recognition, 56, 84, 93, 94, 102
recommendations, 88, 115
recruiting, 87, 114
redistribution, 30
regression, 54
rejection, 57
relevance, 20, 23, 32
rent, 57
replication, 111
requirements, 51
researchers, 3, 35, 38, 39, 40, 42, 46, 49,
   50, 51, 53, 55, 85, 86, 98, 101, 102,
   103, 105, 110, 113

resources, viii, 2, 16, 46, 48, 51, 101, 113
response, 104
restaurants, 27
retirement, 85, 109, 112
revenue, 7, 27, 35, 61
rhythm, 115
risk, ix, 11, 39, 52, 62, 68, 82, 92, 106,
   111
risk factors, 92
risks, 89, 95
rules, 16
rural areas, 58
rural development, 75

S

safety, 87, 104, 114
savings, 110
school, ix, 20, 22, 52, 54, 82, 83, 84, 89,
   92, 95, 96, 97, 98, 99, 100, 101, 102,
   103, 104, 111, 112
school activities, 84, 102
school climate, 104
school success, 95
schooling, 58
science, 34, 93
scope, 4, 15
secondary data, 50, 52
secondary school students, 99
self-control, 98
self-esteem, 52, 106, 109
self-expression, 19, 36, 50
sense of solidarity,, 6
senses, 109
sensory modality, 89
service organizations, 113
services, 67, 74, 111
SES, 83, 94, 98
shape, viii, 14, 81, 96
shortage, 3
showing, ix, 9, 82, 90
Silicon Valley, 71
social behavior, 104

social capital, 58, 109
social consequences, 12
social construct, 36
social infrastructure, 71, 76
social interactions, 84, 107
social network, 109
social psychology, 29
social relations, 83
social sciences, 85, 112
social services, 113
social skills, 13, 28, 52
social support, 12, 20
socialization, 32, 67
societal development,, 5
society, 6, 7, 8, 10, 11, 14, 15, 35, 36, 54, 58, 66, 69, 97, 109
socioeconomic status, 44, 83, 94, 98
software, 7, 15, 27
solidarity, 6
spatial cognition, 83, 94
speech, 7
spending, 7, 26, 33, 67, 74
spillover effects, 61
spirituality, 6, 28
stability, 97
stakeholders, vii, 2, 49, 50
standard deviation, 94
state, 15, 22, 32, 41, 42, 84, 93, 98, 105, 113
states, 14, 15, 29, 64, 103
statistics, 41, 111, 116
stereotypes, 109
stimulation, 110
stock, 15, 49
storytelling, 84, 105, 107, 115
stress, 44, 110
stressors, 92, 95
structural equation modeling, 54
structure, 11, 18, 20, 22, 23, 24, 27, 29, 33, 34, 35, 40, 56, 57, 96
student achievement, 101
subgroups, 32
subjective experience, 103

subjective well-being, 43, 55, 87, 88, 89, 91, 114, 115
subsidies, 15, 16
substance use, 52, 55
substrates, 96
survival, 53
survival rate, 53
suspensions, 52, 84, 100
sustainability, 53
symptoms, 107

T

talent, 51
Task Force, 43, 51
teachers, 92, 93, 100, 101
techniques, 14, 31, 57, 66, 68, 98, 100
technological change, 14
technologies, 103
technology, 20, 104
tensions, 56
testing, 56, 106
theory of system dynamics, 5
therapy, 44, 51
tourism, 6, 7
trade, 56
trade-off, 56
training, 7, 12, 23, 27, 36, 52, 61, 63, 64, 83, 85, 89, 90, 94, 95, 96, 97, 99, 106, 108, 112
traits, 41
transformation, 60, 70
transformations, 13, 28
transition period, 97
traumatic brain injury, 44
treatment, 21, 29, 84, 94, 100, 107, 109
trial, 44, 105

U

U.S. Department of Agriculture, 45
U.S. Department of Labor, 53

U.S. economy, 85, 112
U.S. policy, ix, 81, 88, 104
uniform, 35
United, 13, 41, 91, 101, 102
United Kingdom (UK), 88, 91, 115
United States (USA), 13, 41, 60, 101, 102, 111, 118
universe, 16
universities, 89
urban, 4, 31, 53, 56, 66, 70, 72, 73
urban areas, 56, 67
Urban Institute, 55, 56, 78

V

vacancies, 72
validation, 29
valuation, 74
value chains, 3
variables, viii, 2, 3, 4, 5, 14, 15, 16, 17, 18, 19, 20, 21, 22, 23, 24, 25, 26, 27, 28, 29, 31, 33, 34, 36, 38, 39, 42, 43, 44, 45, 46, 47, 48, 49, 50, 54, 56, 57, 59
variations, 28, 35
vehicles, 15
velocity, 106
venue, 6, 27
verbal fluency, 84, 107

Vice President, 78
visualization, 14
vocabulary, 83, 94, 95
volunteers, 37
voting, 84, 100

W

walking, 106
Washington, 56, 58, 69, 71, 82, 91, 96, 105, 108, 116, 117, 118, 119
web, viii, 41, 76, 81
websites, 54
well-being, viii, 4, 5, 44, 51, 54, 81, 83, 85, 87, 88, 92, 97, 106, 112, 114, 115
wellness, 88, 113
White House, vii, 1, 58, 88, 115
Wisconsin, 77
witnesses, 6
workers, 38, 41, 86, 108
workforce, 58, 85, 97, 109, 112

Y

yield, viii, 39, 41, 42, 43, 45, 52, 81
young adults, 44, 98
young people, 32, 97, 99, 102